The 3G Way:

Dream,

People,

and Culture

An introduction to the management style of Jorge Paulo Lemann, Marcel Telles, and Beto Sicupira, owners of some of the biggest icons of American capitalism

FRANCISCO S. HOMEM DE MELLO

The 3G Way:

Dream, People,

and Culture

"Two years ago my friend, Jorge Paulo Lemann, asked Berkshire to join his 3G Capital group in the acquisition of Heinz. My affirmative response was a no-brainer: I knew immediately that this partnership would work well from both a personal and financial standpoint. And it most definitely has.

"We expect to partner with 3G in more activities. Whatever the structure, we feel good when working with Jorge Paulo."

— Warren Buffet

"This is a management team that does not require shareholder activists."

—Bill Ackman

"Having studied the development of some of the most extraordinary business stories of all time, and the entrepreneurs and leaders who built them, I can say definitely that this story — rising from such humble beginnings to global prominence — is one of which Brazilians should be immensely proud. It stands in the same league as great visionaries like Walt Disney, Henry Ford, Sam Walton, Akio Morita, and Steve Jobs. And it is a story that leaders from around the world should know, as a source of learning and inspiration."

— Jim Collins

"The traditional factors of production—land, labor, and capital—are becoming restraints rather than driving forces. Knowledge is becoming the one critical factor of production."

— Peter F. Drucker

CONTENTS

FOREWORD TO THE 2ND EDITION

This is a revised edition of *The 3G Way*, a book I wrote just after quitting my Executive Director position at one of Brazil's largest investment banks to venture out on my own as an entrepreneur.

Days after leaving my job, I was staring at a blank white board I had installed in my home study to jot down business ideas for my next professional steps. Brainstorming about the two major paths I considered pursuing—a private equity search fund, and a technology venture—I thought hard about the world's greatest practitioners on each field, and quickly came up with two names: 3G Capital, on the private equity side, and Sequoia Capital, on the tech startup side.

I was already familiar with both firms' work. The 3G principals (Jorge Paulo Lemann, Marcel Telles, and Beto Sicupira) are notorious businessmen in Brazil, the subject of a handful of magazine profiles, and a recent book, *Dream Big*, that shows their trajectory through an historical angle. They are the founders of Banco Garantia, a firm which greatly inspired the bank I'd worked for the past six years. They held, among other things, controlling shareholders of AB InBev, which had grown from a small private equity deal of $60 million (the acquisition of Brahma) to become the world's largest brewery after the Anheuser-Busch acquisition for more than $60 billion in cash back in 2008.

Sequoia had also been a great inspiration for me for some time. Since 2012, I'd been investing in tech startups as a micro venture capitalist (basically, putting my bonuses into risky startups—way to go!), and thought constantly about launching my own company. I read everything I could get my hands on about Sequoia's methods and requirements for investing (which provided a great framework with which to start thinking about my own startup[1].)

After reading Jeff Bezos' biography, *The Everything Store*, I was also convinced that there was no better way to test if I'd really learned everything than writing it all down. That's when I first thought about actually publishing a book for my family and friends.

So off I went to research everything about the trio, who are informally referred to as "the 3G," as in the *three Garantia guys*. I watched old interviews, keynote presentations at various university conferences, and even a handful of commencement speeches, where they repeatedly laid out their management style as a very simple triad of a big dream, great, talented people, and a strong culture. I read magazine pieces, and all newspaper clippings I could get my hands on. In the best Lean Startup fashion (something I was also researching at the time), I decided to ship an initial version - MVP[2] - of the book quickly, get

---

[1] Curiously, it ended up being the subject of my first book, Hacking the Startup Investor Pitch: What Sequoia Capital's business plan framework can teach you about building and pitching your company.

[2] Minimum Viable Product

feedback from readers, reinforce what was working, and tweak what wasn't. In July, I pressed "Submit" on Amazon, and leaned back in my chair, thinking, "What the heck have I done?"

It turns out the few friends to whom I had the courage to show the book really liked it. It magically started flying off the "shelves." Fifty thousand sales later, I finally decided to give it a rewrite, incorporating the feedback I'd gotten, and publish a second edition. It's been a great ride, and I am thankful for how much I've learned from this process. It couldn't have been better.

What, then, is different in this new edition? First, my understanding of this fascinating corporate culture has evolved a lot, and frankly, I've barely scratched the surface. Whereas the first edition targeted their culture broadly, the second edition narrows my focus on AB InBev, which in my opinion, turns out to be the best, most sophisticated and refined reflection of the trio's management style. It's the company to which they've dedicated the most time, as it's been under their reign for twenty years, so it's had plenty of time to absorb the Dream, People, and Culture style; and Marcel Telles has personally presided over it for almost ten years. You'll also see that I've taken lots of quotes from their annual reports, a practice that never ceases to amaze me: how incredibly transparent these guys are about their "secret sauce."[3] It's all there, in the open, for anyone to see and replicate. Frankly, I don't see many entrepreneurs devouring these reports like the trio devoured GE's, Goldman Sachs's, and Walmart's reports back in the day. I'll leave you, the reader, to ponder that, from which powerful conclusions may arise.

I've also given a lot of thought to the book's title. Although it's called *The 3G Way* because 3G is a proxy for the trio's names, I didn't want it to look like it was a book about 3G Capital, which is an increasingly important, but very recent, undertaking of theirs. *Dream, People, Culture* would be a title more truthful to their management style and history. That's why I decided to merge both and title this version *The 3G Way: Dream, People, and Culture.*

Lastly, today, as I headed home today to write this prologue, I was bombarded by messages from

---

[3] No Heinz-related puns intended.

friends wanting to know if I'd have time to include "the deal" in this version. *What deal!?* I couldn't ask them, or my "expert" mask would fall in front of them. As I desperately tried to Google the Wall Street Journal, my car broke down, and I was stranded for hours on end with no data signal to end my desperate quest for information. It was only when I sat down to write this, hours later, that I learned about the Heinz-Kraft merger, and couldn't stop from feeling proud about my work: even though it was an obvious target for the 3G, I take great pleasure in knowing that they are increasing their bets on Kraft's breed of company, a theme to which I've dedicated a subchapter in the book's introduction.

I hope you enjoy it!

Francisco S. Homem de Mello
São Paulo, March 25, 2015

FOREWORD TO THE 1ST EDITION

Before telling you what this book is, I am going to tell you what it is not.

It is not intended as a comprehensive management manual; it's not intended as a definitive guide; it's not intended as a biographic account; it's not intended as cheesy, entertaining business nonfiction. It is meant to provide you a door into the methods applied by the 3G that I hope will give you some management ideas to apply, and inspire you to research the 3G Way further.

In being true to 3G's philosophy, I have kept the book as short and as simple as possible. I am just trying to bring a little more color and detail to the methods Jorge Paulo himself has repeatedly reduced to "hard work and discipline." For the sake of your time, and mine as well, I have also avoided current trends in business nonfiction, such as telling stories for every single point I wanted to make. Although it makes the read more entertaining, it sounds manufactured and takes up precious reader time that should be spent in applying the content anyway.

I based this material on various public sources, including videos recorded for Stanford Graduate School of Business and Endeavor; magazine articles from HSM, Fortune, Forbes, and other top-notch business publications; books; and informal talks with a dozen or so former employees of Banco, Garantia, AB Inbev, Burger King, and 3G Capital. In doing so, I hoped to form a cohesive view of their method, while keeping the text as objective as possible.

I received no help from the trio on my research. The most I got, from Jorge Paulo himself, was a hint that I was on the right track. This is easily justifiable: first, I am a newbie author and second, they have historically shunned any publicity. Nonetheless, I think the management world would greatly benefit from a more complete and technical account of their practices.

Lastly, I write this from a position of great admiration for the success these three Brazilians have achieved in business. I have worked in great companies and bad companies, and know firsthand the challenges that management presents. It's much harder to produce the kind of stellar results they have than it seems. Second, I feel proud for them being Brazilians, a private sector that has frequently thrived despite serious macroeconomic headwinds, corruption, a bizarre tax code, and an even worse legal framework.

So I hope you enjoy this

.

A BIT OF HISTORY

Garantia: a partnership from the tropics

Garantia was the first big venture of Jorge Paulo Lemann, a Swiss-Brazilian who holds a Bachelor's degree in economics from Harvard, and whose passion for tennis led him to represent Brazil in the famed Davis Cup. He purchased the little-known Rio de Janeiro-based broker dealer in 1971 with financing from family and friends. In 1976, after rejecting an acquisition offer from J.P. Morgan, he transformed it into a full-fledged investment bank.

Garantia was openly inspired by Goldman Sachs, the New York-based investment bank known as the most successful Wall Street partnership in history. The firm, which is a bank holding company nowadays, worked then as a private partnership, wholly held by its executives, who were annually invited to increase or decrease their holdings based on their work performance.

The model worked well for the investment banking business back then: mergers and acquisitions, equity and debt underwriting, and sales and trading were all capital-light businesses that provided huge return-on-equity for these firms. Later on, placement guarantees, bridge loans, and increasing competition led them to raise larger, more permanent capital from investors, a movement that culminated with Goldman's IPO in the 1990s.

The firm was such an inspiration to Lemann that he managed to get his partner, Luiz Cezar Fernandes, who would later found Banco Pactual

(BTG Pactual these days,) an internship there, to learn Goldman's ways. Fernandes found himself an aide, Marcel Hermann Telles, a newly hired analyst at the bank, to be his translator[4]. In Lemann's words, "with Goldman we learned meritocracy, intense employee training, and the need to give people growth opportunities," which remain strong traits of their culture to this day.

The audacity to ask for such "internships" as a way of benchmarking the world's best business practices would be a trademark of the trio. They replicated the tactic with Walmart and Anheuser-Busch to great success.

The trio's third member, Carlos Alberto "Beto" da Veiga Sicupira, joined Garantia in 1973, a year after Marcel, after having met Lemann at a spearfishing getaway with mutual friends.

---

[4] Telles would go on, alongside Lemann, to control AB InBev, Burger King, and Heinz, as well as multiple other businesses.

Lojas Americanas: the trio's first incursion into private equity

In 1982, after a number of small-time investments in publicly traded stocks like Lojas Brasileiras and São Paulo Alpargatas, Garantia undertook the first hostile takeover in the São Paulo Stock Exchange (Bovespa), purchasing a controlling stake in Lojas Americanas for approximately 20 million dollars.

Nowadays, such a maneuver would be economically infeasible in Brazilian markets. Publicly-traded corporation's entrenched minority shareholders protect themselves with layers of poison pills and golden parachutes, forcing hostile bidders to make offers for the whole company and pay large sums to executives and boards.

The trio always found great opportunities in companies that lack clear, present owners to direct them. They become fertile ground for agent-principal conflicts of interest, where executives' incentives become misaligned with shareholders'.

These companies tend to present lackluster financial and operational performances, and fail to attract and retain top talent, as Lemann highlights in an interview to HSM Management magazine in 2008[5]:

> We basically think that ideal companies are the ones that are publicly traded, but that also have shareholders working for them, because they are surely interested in the really long-term, and in perpetuating the business. I think that's the ideal balance for a good, long-lasting company. I've been myself a part of many an American company's board of directors where nobody's got more than 2%, or 3% of the stock. Results were ok, but in general executives start to run the show, and that doesn't seem healthy, because it generates an environment of excessive stock option issuance, compensation, and attention to quarterly earnings. In sum, my ideal company is not one that lacks a clear owner. I prefer InBev's current model, where several

---

[5] Translated by the author.

shareholders take part in the company's management, ensuring really long-term focus, and also the public shareholders, executives, and employees, who've got generous stock purchasing packages.

Marcel Telles, speaking at Endeavor's 2013 CEO Summit[6], adds to the view, highlighting the opportunities that arise from lack of ownership coupled with strong brands and competitive advantages:

[We look for] companies that are extraordinary in spite of those executives who're in and out every three years, of not having owners for a number of generations. They have to have something: a strong brand, a distribution system, a franchise, something that enables them to survive and still be excelente. Usually, these companies are in boring sectors, that don't carry the charm of Wall Street, of Silicon Valley... These companies don't attract top talent anymore.

[6] You may find all the videos cited throughout the book at http://www.the3gway.com/videos

Lojas Americanas, the Brazilian variety retailer, was the perfect example: principal-agent misalignment had led to sub-optimal results, in the trio's view. That led them to try to replicate their management style—then restricted to Garantia's small financial partnership—in the real economy. The trio also welcomed some asset diversification, since their net worths then were totally committed to the markets.

Beto, who's described by some as "a bulldozer," was designated to leave Garantia and run the new company. He allegedly shocked his new colleagues when he first arrived dressed in jeans and carrying a backpack that made him look like a college student. The company had a very austere culture back then, with wood-paneled private offices and a luxurious corporate restaurant for its management. The shock didn't end there: Beto instituted new performance guidelines, questioned ongoing practices, abolished private offices in favor of an open-plan shared space, and installed an argumentative, informal working culture similar to the bank.

In no time, he had to face a riot within the company's management, who threatened to quit if the status quo wasn't reinstated. After a few hours of reflection (and maybe a couple of calls to his partners at Garantia), Beto fired the rebellious subordinates, arguing that acting quickly and decisively was paramount in (re)building the company's culture. Under his rule, Americanas's payroll went from more than 14,000 employees to around 8,000.

In 1993, Beto founded GP Investimentos (currently GP Investments), a private equity-focused asset management firm that raised its first fund ($500 million) in 1994, and eventually held stakes in important companies such as GloboCabo, Telemar, and ALL (América Latina Logística), as well as in many companies that today comprise Americanas.com, Lojas Americanas e-tailing spin-off. The firm is currently run by two second-generation executives, Antonio Bonchristiano, founder of dot-com star Submarino, and Fersen Lambranho, former CEO of Lojas Americanas.

Brahma and the brewing business

The year of 1989 brought the game-changing acquisition of Brahma, a Rio de Janeiro-based brewery, for $60 million. It was a controversial transaction amongst Garantia partners for its size, complexity, and timing. The acquisition came just months before the historic election of Fernando Collor de Mello against then-union leader Luiz Inácio "Lula" da Silva, who scared Brazilian businessmen with his harsh left-wing stances.

In hindsight, Lemann credits the trio's guts with the decision to proceed with the deal in such dire times, and without the proper financial and legal due diligence. Days after the closing, a large hole in the company's pension plan surfaced, one that would've probably caused the trio to back away had it been known in advance. In Lemann's words,

> *Our feelings told us to go ahead, because we were a young, tropical country, and we really believed the beer business was a good one, being poorly managed. That was more important than Lula or Collor winning the elections, or if there was a hole or not in the pension plan.*

Marcel Telles, who years before had accompanied his boss during the Goldman internship, was designated to run the company and become its CEO. As expected, he implemented a management revolution, with methods refined from the Garantia and Lojas Americanas experiences. He went on to expand the company's footprint to Argentina, Uruguay, and Venezuela, and to start improving Brahma's manufacturing practices with the help of Vicente Falconi, founder of Falconi Consultores de Resultado (we'll see more of this in a bit).

After ten years, Marcel relayed the bat to Magim Rodriguez, who'd met the trio years before as an executive of chocolate producer Lacta (currently Mondelez), a supplier of Americanas. But Marcel nonetheless orchestrated the acquisition of Brahma's archrival, Antarctica—a São Paulo-based brewery—from his new post in the board of directors. The deal, which years before would have been a merger of equals, turned out to be an acquisition by the much larger Brahma, and led the trio to share the company's control with Fundação Zerrener, Antarctica's controlling shareholder.

The resulting company was named AmBev, as in American Beverage Company, and would go on to dominate 70% of the Brazilian beer market (and 40% of the overall beverage market.)

The best part of those first ten years heading Brahma had been taken by Marcel's efforts to build an all-star team at the company. He would call them "The Few. The Proud," in an allusion to the

U.S. Marine Corps slogan. One of them was Carlos Brito, who'd come from Garantia after a Lemann-financed Stanford MBA degree, and took responsibility for one of the company's plants. This team was essential in the integration of Antarctica's operations, an antithesis of Brahma back then: executives had huge private offices that were luxuriously ornate, and the C-suite was a collection of old-school cotton heads.

Another decisive factor was the management framework brought by Falconi, then a management professor at Universidade Federal de Minas Gerais's Christiano Ottoni Foundation, where he taught Total Quality Management and Toyota Production System-inspired management tools. In the following decades, Falconi (along with AmBev's executives) would develop most of the company's goals-based management system and manufacturing practices, part of a complete methodology that would come to be adopted by a number of Brazil's largest corporations as well as by the Aécio Neves-led Minas Gerais state government.

For a better idea of how much Marcel and Falconi impacted Brahma's productivity, the company contributed half of the workforce to the combined entity, AmBev, while at the same time being accountable to two thirds of the joint output in terms of volume. Productivity per manufacturing employee was 8.776 hectoliters in 1999, and in 2000, the first year of combined operations, it jumped back to 7.556 hectoliters, a slump that would be quickly reversed by Rodriguez and team.

This management style, which is observably consistent over the years as per the company's annual reports, was neatly captured by AmBev's 2002 letter to shareholders, which was signed by the co-chairmen of AmBev's board, Telles and Vitório De Marchi (who represented the interests of Fundação Zerrener), and by Rodriguez, then general manager

The essence of our company is, and will continue to be, in our management capabilities, our culture, and our people's unparalleled execution. We select, train, and follow carefully our young talents' careers. We are all confident and demanding.

We are motivated by an aggressive variable compensation system, which stimulates high performance, accountability, and entrepreneurship. Everybody at AmBev is focused in reaching long-term, sustainable goals. Strict financial discipline is intrinsic to our culture.

We're a young company, with an average age of 29 years. Nonetheless, we're also a very capable management team. Senior executives take active part in recruiting the best professionals, carefully breeding the company's next generation of ranks.

These basic principles are supported by our talent, the AmBev people, by our proprietary processes, and by the unique way we make things happen.[7]

The Interbrew deal: the trio goes global

From 1999 to 2004, the Antarctica integration, which involved creating an integrated services center (CSC, or Centro de Serviços Compartilhados) to render administrative services to the company's many plants and distribution centers, didn't slow AmBev down from its Latin American expansion.

---

[7] "A essência de nossa Companhia é, e continuará sendo, nossa capacidade gerencial, nossa cultura e a capacidade sem paralelos de execução da nossa gente. Selecionamos, treinamos e acompanhamos, cuidadosamente, jovens talentos. Somos todos confiantes e exigentes.

Somos motivados por um agressivo sistema de remuneração variável que estimula o desempenho, a responsabilidade e o espírito empreendedor. Todos na AmBev estão focados em atingir resultados sustentáveis de longo prazo. Rigidez e disciplina financeira são componentes da nossa cultura.

Somos uma empresa jovem onde a idade média é 29 anos. Entretanto, somos um time com grande capacidade gerencial. Os altos executivos participam ativamente do processo de seleção dos melhores profissionais no mercado, cuidadosamente preparando a próxima geração de executivos.

Esses princípios básicos são suportados por pessoas talentosas, a gente AmBev, pelos nossos processos proprietários e pela maneira única com que fazemos as coisas acontecerem."

The strategy was to start greenfield operations on most relevant markets of the region, while keeping an eye out for opportunistic acquisitions. Following this directive, it acquired Quinsa, the owner of the Argentina-based beer brand Quilmes, in 2003; two of the largest Pepsi bottlers in Peru; and other similar smaller transactions, like a joint venture with the largest Pepsi bottler in Central America.

The Latin American expansion spree wasn't enough to quench the trio's thirst. In 2004, in the midst of a global wave of consolidation, AmBev considered its merger options amongst other large players. Anheuser Busch and Heineken were not good options: their sheer size would engulf AmBev, leaving little room for the trio's commitment to retaining control of the company. SAB Miller, from South Africa, and Interbrew, from Belgium, were on the size/geographic footprint sweet spot, and therefore given more consideration.

DREAM, PEOPLE, CULTURE

In March 2004, AmBev and its controlling shareholders announced a complex transaction, in which the trio, via its Braco holding company, merged its controlling stake in AmBev with a number of Belgium-based families' stakes in Interbrew. As a result, the trio would share control in the combined company, which would itself hold controlling stakes in both AmBev[8] and Interbrew, and be called InBev[9].

AmBev's talent factory, spilling out droves of highly-talented executives at full speed, was able to expatriate more than one hundred executives of all seniority levels to international outposts of the

---

[8] AmBev's minority shareholders were left out of the deal: they remained only AmBev shareholders, with no stakes in InBev whatsoever. AmBev, would come to own all of the groups American assets until the AB acquisition: Labatt, the Canadian operation, was sold, as part of the deal, to AmBev, which in turn issued additional shares in InBev's favour.

[9] Lemann, Telles, and Sicupira kept a 24.7% stake in InBev's voting shares, and signed a shareholders' agreement with the Belgium families that ensured them "joint influence, in equal terms" over the company's decisions.

newly-created company. Carlos Brito, AB InBev's current CEO, was one of them: he left AmBev to run Labatt for some time, and to get some international mileage under his belt, a move agreed upon with the Belgians before he took over as InBev's CEO in Leuven.

In the following years, AmBev would do still more M&A activity in Latin America, such as the acquisition of remaining stakes of Quinsa left in the hands of minority shareholders.

Anheuser-Busch

In 2008, InBev started talks to acquire Anheuser Busch, the American brewing icon that owned such traditional brands as Budweiser (the world's most recognized beer brand) and Bud Light. The transaction, led by Carlos Brito under the trio's supervision, was widely criticized by the Busch Family, who ran the company; the U.S. press, who steadfastly opposed foreign companies scooping up American icons; and even by the then-U.S. presidential candidate, Barack Obama. The deal went through despite everything that was working against it.

Rumors of a potential deal went all the way back to 2006, when August Busch IV agreed to distribute InBev's brands in the U.S.A. against the advice of his father, former AB CEO August Busch III.

The distribution deal gave InBev an incredible vantage point into AB's operations: the company went as far as to open an advance base across the street from Anheuser-Busch's St. Louis downtown offices. Carlos Brito was able to peek into the company's many inefficiencies and weaknesses, and he liked what he saw.

Ever since their acquisition of Brahma, the trio had dreamed of owning Budweiser. It was not only the world's largest brewery, but also had what was probably the world's best portfolio of beer brands. To make it an even more attractive target, AB possessed a tripod of (1) meager financial and (2) operational results, as well as (3) diffused stock ownership.

Contrary to what most people thought at the time, the Busch family held less than 10% of Anheuser-Busch's capital: an amount that would get them a seat at the board at most. But despite the little ownership they held, Busch the Fourth and the Third exerted almost complete influence over AB's board, a feat that ensured them the top executive post at the company for a number of decades. The

Buschs acted as the sole owners of the St. Louis-based brewer, extracting what most thought were benefits disproportionate to their small stakes. As Julie Macintosh noted in her *Dethroning the King*:

> *They had never been known for cost-consciousness. For decades, the aviation-loving Busch men and other staffers had hopscotched around the country on the company's own fleet of sleek, leather-outfitted Dassault Falcon corporate jets. It got to the point for a while where even the wives of strategic committee members hadn't flown commercial in years.*

A quote by a former executive interviewed by Macintosh illustrates the Buschs' weak position in relation to their relatively small stake. They could exert influence while nobody questioned their weak ownership status:

> *They were just the titular heads of the company. They didn't have control. It was like a monarchy in Great Britain. These guys really didn't have the authority to do anything.*

After a number of strategic missteps by Busch the Fourth, the market resumed speculations about a possible deal between AB and InBev. In one such misstep, Busch IV had dinner with Lemann in New York, and failed to report to his board the fact that the Brazilian had made an outright, albeit informal, proposal to combine the two companies in some way.

Feeling his idea wasn't taken seriously by Busch the Fourth, Lemann and his partners started considering a hostile takeover of the company. (In a hostile offer, the acquiring company by-passes the target's board of directors by approaching shareholders directly. In contrast, friendly acquirers usually approach the target's board first. The board analyzes the offer, and only recommends it to its shareholders after approving the deal.)

Everything pointed to the fact that AB's board, dominated by the Third and the Fourth, would do little to get a deal with InBev done. It would disrupt their luxurious status quo and expose years of management inefficiencies to the world.

An alternative course of action was to approach the board, but make it public by "leaking" copies to the press, and in the process creating an environment where it would be embarrassing not to seriously consider the offer, which was AB's board of directors' fiduciary duty in the first place. InBev ended up using just such a course of action.

The first formal bid was relayed to AB on July 11th, 2008, with a price tag of $65 per AB share, valuing the company at $46.3 billion. On July 1st, after having sent three public letters to AB's board, and having its offer rejected on the grounds of being "financially inadequate" and not in the best interest of its shareholders, InBev reinforced its $65 per share bid, and started discussing the removal of several AB board members. On July 7th, InBev went even further, and filed a preliminary proposal with the SEC (Securities and

Exchange Commission, regulator of American financial markets) to oust the AB board. AB finally acquiesced on the 11th of July, and started "friendly" negotiations with the Belgium-based company, which ended up raising the price to $70 per share, or $52 billion, to be paid in cash to its shareholders.

To fund the gigantic deal, InBev had by then secured a large debt facility with a syndicate of banks that agreed to lend it more than $40 billion. To ensure that the group couldn't back down from the commitment, and possibly eyeing the upcoming credit crisis that was deteriorating daily, InBev paid the syndicate an up-front fee of around $50 million, which kept the funding in place even after the bankruptcy of Lehman Brothers, in September 2008.

InBev, on the other hand, seized the once-in-a-lifetime opportunity and didn't back off from the acquisition. Weeks later, it would prove to have happened close to the peak of the markets.

Burger-King, Heinz, and 3G Capital

In 2004, the trio decided to diversify its financial holdings, and seeded 3G Capital, an alternative asset management company to be based in New York. Alex Behring, who'd been a partner at GP Investimentos and went on to head ALL (América Latina Logística, one of the firm's most successful holdings), led the initiative.

3G started out trading in liquid markets and allocating capital in third-party managers via a fund-of-funds. Later on, the firm concentrated its efforts on making large, concentrated investments in publicly traded companies, commonly known as PIPEs (private investment in public equities.)

The first large bet was made in conjunction with TCI, a London-based asset manager led by Chris Hohn and known for a number of activist incursions, namely ABN Amro Bank and the Deutsche Borse. 3G and TCI both acquired a large stake in CSX, an American railroad company, and pressed for aggressive changes in the company's management. They were partially backed by Behring's experience in ALL, Brazil's largest railroad operator.

After CSX, 3G raised a new fund enabling it to announce the take-private of Burger King in 2010. The fast-food chain was then held by private equity funds run by the Texas Pacific Group, Bain Capital, and Goldman Sachs, who'd purchased the company from Diageo in 2002. The group was having trouble running it, especially after the 2008 recession. The buyout valued BK at $3.3 billion (plus $700 million in debts), or nine times earnings. The disbursement was levered roughly one-to-one, which added around $1.7 billion of takeover debt on top of the existing $700 million. Bernardo Hees, who'd succeeded Behring as CEO of ALL, was named CEO, followed by Daniel Schwartz, who'd led the deal for 3G, as CFO.

In 2012, after less than two years at the head of the company, Hees merged it with Justice Holdings, a special purpose acquisition company (SPAC) owned by Pershing Square Capital Management[10] funds. 3G and its investors received $1.4 billion in cash (approximately what they had invested in equity in the first place) and 70% of the combined company's shares. BK was then incorporated into the acquiring vehicle, and became itself publicly traded, a transaction commonly known as a reverse-IPO.

With both CSX and Burger King successes in its curriculum, 3G Capital, which counts Jorge Paulo

---

[10] Pershing Square is a New York-based asset management firm dedicated to activist investments: buying relevant stakes in public companies, and then using a variety of methods (from friendly talks, to public letters to management, to proxy fights for board seats) to press for management/strategic changes.

Lemann, Beto Sicupira, and Marcel Telles as its "principals," went on to join forces with Warren Buffet (who'd been a Gillette board member alongside Lemann), to take over H.J. Heinz Company, manufacturer of the famous namesake ketchup brand. The deal was significantly larger than the previous ones, but followed the same framework: overtaking a large, U.S.-based, public company private, using large amounts of cheap debt. Heinz shareholders received $23.3 billion in cash.

The common thread

It's clear, by the trio's business trajectory that they were getting more and more focused on a very narrow specialty of transactions. Here are three common threads between the companies they allocate most of their time and money to nowadays (only confirmed by the announced deal to merge Kraft and Heinz).

a) *Focus on developed markets*

Since merging their stakes with Interbrew, the trio has increasingly concentrated their efforts on developed markets like the U.S. and Europe. These markets present a unique combination of factors which suit their skills:

- Many public companies with diffuse ownership, which they consider a huge handicap for company performance.

- Abundant and cheap debt leverage to finance their deals.

- Stable economic and political environments in which to base their companies, with significant geographic diversification of revenues and exogenous risk factors (inflation, interest rates, economic growth, geo-political risk, and so on).

They haven't closed a single relevant deal in Brazil, their home turf, in the past 10 years.

b) *Companies with above-average competitive advantages*

Despite believing that the dream-people-culture tripod is the only truly sustainable competitive advantage, the trio still looks for companies that thrive (albeit sub-optimally) despite its absence, as we'll see in more detail. Factors they seek could include strong brands, distribution systems, low supplier/customer concentration, and little technological disruption risk.

c) *Large potential efficiency gains*

Businesses like the manufacturing and sale of Fast-Moving Consumer Goods (FMCGs)—for instance, beers, burgers, and sauces—all carry high production costs, of which labor is a significant part. These can be streamlined with their management style for substantial margin improvements.

d) *High margins*

Again, producing and selling FMCGs is a high-margin trade (when compared to pure retail, for example) and is forgiving to large amounts of financial leverage.

e) *Idiot-proof sectors*

Relative competitive advantages are not enough if the business sector is not structurally sound and structurally forgiving.

The trio's departure from investment banking—the sale of Banco Garantia—is very illustrative: they left behind a very high-maintenance business, where there's little scalability, high market-risk exposure, and significant dependence on key personnel, to focus on FMCGs. They've followed Warren Buffet's famous tenet: "I try to buy stocks in businesses that are so wonderful that an idiot can run them. Because sooner or later, one will."

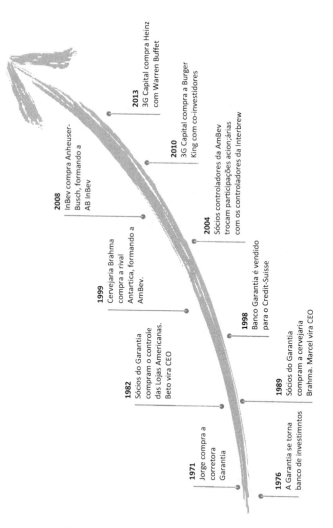

Figure 1: The trio's timeline.

DREAM, PEOPLE, CULTURE

Select Financial Performance

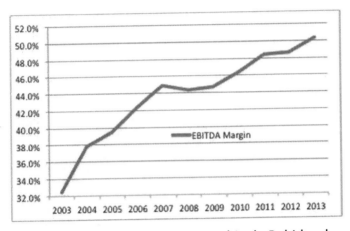

Figure 2: EBITDA Margin - Companhia de Bebidas das Américas (AmBev), 2003–2013.

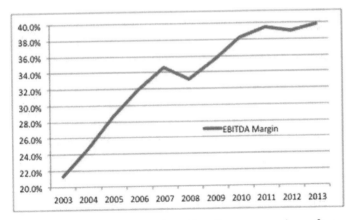

Figure 3: EBITDA Margin – Pro-forma numbers for Interbrew, Inbev e AB Inbev, 2003–2013.

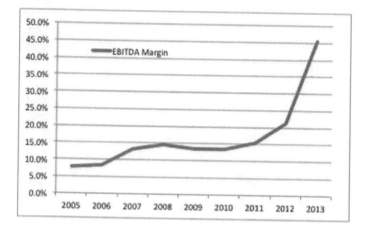

Figure 4: EBITDA Margin - Burger King,
2005 – 2013.

PART 1: PEOPLE

Foreword on People

A company's biggest asset is good people working as a team, growing in proportion to their talent and being recognized for that. Employee compensation has to be aligned with shareholders' interests.

– The 18 Commandments

Our commitment to recruiting, training, and retaining our best people is a key element of our strategic initiatives. We know the AmBev People are our greatest competitive advantage.

–AmBev's 2003 Annual Report

We're a one-trick-pony: our trick is to leverage people. That's what we know how to do. Find people that have talent, a spark in their eyes, and a desire to grow, and open up their path, to help them get ahead.

–Marcel Telles

According to Carlos Brito, in his "View from the Top" presentation at Stanford in 2011, "Great people are what forms great companies." For a company to be great, the majority of its people have to be great: there is no other magical ingredient.

It sounds incredibly simple. But it is not!

In order to have great people, a company has to invest in several fronts:

- Foster an environment where great people feel great.

- Create a constant pipeline for great people to enter and climb the company's ranks.

- Compensate great people disproportionately.

- Get rid of the poorest performers, so that the average talent pool improves constantly.

According to Brito, great people like working for companies that have three key traits:

- Meritocracy: the best are recognized and the worst are driven out of the system.

- Informality: hierarchy is not imposed, but earned, and where they can express their opinions openly without peer pressure and political concerns.

- Candor: there are no hidden agendas. Fact-based discussions and a clear notion of where people stand in the company is the rule and not the exception.

Besides having an environment that pleases great people, it is very important that the company has a constant pipeline of talent in all its ranks. That's done in many ways.

First of all, supply the base of the pyramid with fresh talent via internship, trainee, and MBA programs, all over the globe. AB InBev's senior management all get involved in the final steps of the recruiting process, ensuring cultural fit and getting the best people on board personally.

The best people move up from the base quickly, being constantly rewarded for their top-notch performance and receiving loads of training related to these new responsibilities. Leaders are all required to have at least two team members identified as potential successors, from which at least one must be ready to take on the position within the next six months. This ensures that most of the higher-ups running AB InBev today were at the bottom of the organizational chart at one point, and that they are 100% fit for the company's unique culture.

As simple and straightforward as these concepts sound to business managers, their implementation takes utmost discipline and focus.

Especially during the transition toward an informal, candid meritocracy, those people Carlos Brito refers to as mediocre (a harsh but candid term) will be very displeased with the new way of doing things. Nice people who have worked for a company for a very long time will no longer feel safe and warm in their corners, and others won't like the competitive environment, in which employees constantly challenge their peer's views and assumptions. Again, it is always easier to kick the can down the road and maintain the status quo, but these changes are the foundation of a great company.

FRANCISCO S. HOMEM DE MELLO

1

Meritocracy: Easy to grasp, hard to execute

Meritocracy: a system in which the talented are chosen and moved ahead on the basis of their achievement.

— Merriam-Webster Dictionary

True meritocracy is probably the most important and distinctive aspect of the trio's management style, and can best be understood as treating differently-performing people differently, compensating the best disproportionately, and dealing honestly with poor performers, either by coaching them to improve, or by firing them.

The backbone of a meritocracy is a variable compensation system backed by individualized goals and performance reviews. Variable compensation comes in two forms: money and promotions/responsibility.

Meritocracy in school and sports

According to Brito, we are introduced to meritocracies early on, in school. Grades are usually public and very objective, and people have to pull their own weight to get ahead. Later on, we get involved with sports, which are also meritocracies: we get to play if we are good; we get to sit on the bench if we are mediocre. Coaches offer constant feedback and apply a healthy dose of pressure.

The corporate world: where meritocracy gets disrupted

Executives, on the other hand, often take a host of other factors into account when managing their employees: time on the job, personal ties of friendship, and loyalty to the company. But this works like a cancer, because it shows people that regardless of how much great work they produce, they are not going to be recognized for it. What follows is a deathly spiral, as the performance of the majority of associates degenerates significantly. The feedback loop feeds itself into an obit certificate[11].

According to Carlos Brito, being meritocratic is not easy. Dealing with poor performance, for example, takes manager discipline to face the facts, confront the employee, and fire him or her after three

---

[11] Not only are the wrong employees frequently promoted, but the good employees feel so demotivated that they leave to other companies, intensifying the problem.

feedback sessions have not brought about the intended performance improvement. But it is what's best, for both the company *and* the employee: the company will be able to promote a performer to fill the vacant role, while the employee will be able to tweak his or her career to pursue work that is a better personal fit. Still referring to poor performances, Brito states, "Yes, there will be people at the bottom. And that's the idea; that people at the bottom feel bad, and they want to go to the top." Letting employees know how their performance relates to their colleagues' achievements fosters healthy competition.

Jack Welch, a huge influence to AB InBev's culture, seems to agree, as can be seen in his 2002 GE Annual Report:

> *Not removing that bottom 10% [of worse performers] early in their careers is not only a management failure, but false kindness as well – a form of cruelty – because inevitably a new leader will come into a business and*

take out that bottom 10% right away, leaving them –
sometimes midway through a career – stranded and
having to start over somewhere else.

What is merit?

Defining merit is tough. At first glance, merit is "delivering the numbers," which is basically hitting your goals. But that's only a third of the tripod used to define the key traits of an ideal leader:

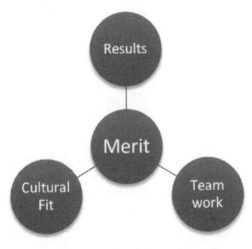

Figure 5: Leadership and merit.

Making the numbers

Delivery is a very objective concept that is widely measured within the company. What's the employee's weighted average of goals hit? Different goals have different weights, and each employee's goal has a percentage of completion measured by the start of every performance review.

When the employee doesn't hit his numbers (70% is the absolute minimum), it's up to his or her leader to assess if he or she needs training, if the goals were not set appropriately, or if the employee is just plain wrong for the function.

Teamwork

Teamwork is measured by leaders and a formal 360-degree annual review. What's the professional's ability to work with a team, motivate their direct reports, create no trouble, and breed talent within the ranks?

Those who have teamwork issues but do deliver the numbers and have cultural fit may be directed to specific training programs directed at "prima donnas." They're given some time to work on their weaknesses.

Cultural fit

Cultural fit is the only leg of the tripod that is absolutely non-negotiable. Values such as integrity, meritocracy, ownership mindset, and the pursuit of excellence are not a matter of training, and are deal breakers.

GE, again in its 2002 Annual Report, explains a framework very much alike AB InBev's:

It's about the four 'types' that represent the way we evaluate and deal with our existing leaders.

Type I: shares our values; makes the numbers – sky's the limit!

Type II: doesn't share the values; doesn't make the numbers – gone.

Type III: shares the values; misses the numbers — typically, another chance, or two.

None of these three are tough calls, but Type IV is the toughest call of all: the manager who doesn't share the values, but delivers the numbers; the 'go-to' manager, the hammer, who delivers the bacon but does it on the backs of people, often "kissing up and kicking down" during the process. This type is the toughest to part with because organizations always want to deliver — it's in the blood — and to let someone go who gets the job done is yet another unnatural act. But we have to remove these Type IVs because they have the power, by themselves, to destroy the open, informal, trust-based culture we need to win today and tomorrow.

Performance reviews: putting meritocracy to practice

Performance reviews are the foundation of every meritocracy, and at AB InBev, it is divided into three main parts:

Page 60

1 Monthly numbers review

2 Mid-year formal review

3 Annual formal review and bonus

Monthly numbers reviews are meetings that a leader holds with his or her direct reports, aiming to review each person's numbers and goals (including the leader's), and deciding course corrections for those who are straying from their targets. Colleagues are encouraged to jump into each other's discussions, suggesting causes and solutions to problems, and sharing best practices.

In the middle of each year, each leader conducts a one-on-one meeting with his or her direct reports, where a more comprehensive discussion of results and goals is performed, as well as any relevant feedback better suited to a private conversation. There are hardly any surprises in these reviews, since the numbers are very openly discussed monthly, so this is a place for deeper feedback, especially negative, and for a recovery action plan, which has to have 5Ws and 1H:

- what is to be done
- by whom
- until when
- where
- why, and finally
- how.

Finally, by year end the formal one-on-one review is undertaken: leader and report sit for another round of results, goals, and feedback, after which the individual performance number will be set. The individual performance number, or index, is the weighted average of the percentage of completion of all of the person's goals:

Goal 1: Raising sales by 10% (Weight of 70%)

Goal 2: Increasing # of client visits by 5% (Weight of 30%)

Let's say this hypothetical employee has hit his first goal, but has hit only 50% of the 2nd goal. Her final performance index will be

I.P. = (100%*70%) + (50%*30%) = 70% + 15% = 85%

This process is undertaken by the whole firm, from the CEO down to the lower managerial posts. Reports provide leaders with their goals, results, challenges, and action plans. Leaders then provide reports with feedback, coaching, suggestions, tools, resources, and knowledge.

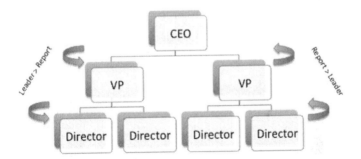

Figure 6: Performance review process.

Variable compensation

Variable compensation happens differently for different management functions (bonus based on performance reviews) and operational roles (bonus based on collective excellence programs).

Management Bonus

Every year, management employees are eligible to earn a bonus: a product of his/her individual performance, the collective performance of his team, and the overall company performance.

Individual Performance	x	Team Performance	x	Company Performance

We already know that the Individual Performance index is a function of the employee's results. Team performance, as we'll see in further detail on the goals chapter, is how the team as a whole fared relative to its goals. If every professional in the team made his or her numbers, then logically the team will have made its numbers, because individual goals are necessarily broken down from collective goals, which are themselves broken down from firm-wide goals. Firm-wide goals follow the same logic.

So it doesn't matter if the individual had great performance for the year: he or she will be punished if their team doesn't collectively make its goals, and the same goes for the firm. This process leads to a great alignment of interests among employees and shareholders, who all ultimately benefit from the same outcomes.

After everyone is graded with their performance indexes (as we saw, the performance index is an overall percentage of goal completion), management goes on to rank all employees in a forced curve, which historically has the shape of a bell graph, to get them their final bonus grades.

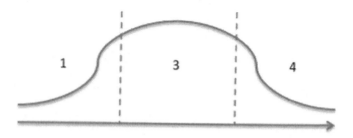

1 = ~30% of employees ; Bonus = 0 x base salary
3 = ~50% of employees ; Bonus = 2 x base salary
4 = ~15% of employees ; Bonus = 3 x base salary

Figure 7: The relative performance curve.

At the bottom of the curve are the Ones, who have sub-par performance. Ideally, the bottom 10% should be fired immediately. Their presence there is usually not a matter of circumstance, but of repeated bad performance. Moving them on gives fresh people a try at those jobs, and the employee a shot at finding a better-suited career.

Threes are the core of the company. Their performance is great, but they're either not ready for a promotion, or are some of those experts who are excellent at what they do, but don't have many managerial ambitions (great accountants and lawyers may fit the bill.) Note that if the company is constantly shaving the worst performers, Threes constantly have to improve their relative performance, or risk becoming Ones. This mechanic ensures that the talent pool is constantly striving to improve, fueled with a healthy dose of lateral competition.

Fours are the movers: excellent employees who're on a path of excelling at everything they tackle, and who are very ambitious about growing within the ranks. These must get an outsized portion of the company's "love and care" in the form of bonuses, promotions, training, etc.

You may be wondering about the missing 5%, or the Two category on the graph: these are the employees that have been at their jobs for less than six months, and thus are not eligible for performance reviews. The company gives them leeway to settle into their new jobs and get their grips.

A very similar practice can be found in GE, a great inspiration for the trio, as is made clear by the company's 2002 Annual Report:

In every evaluation and reward system, we break our population down into three categories: the top 20%, the high-performance middle 70% and the bottom 10%. The top 20% must be loved, nurtured, and rewarded in the soul and wallet, because they are the ones who make magic happen. Losing one of these people must be held up as a leadership sin – a real failing.

The top 20% and middle 70% are not permanent labels. People move between them all the time. However, the bottom 10%, in our experience, tend to remain there. A company that bets its future on its people must remove that lower 10%, and keep removing it every year: always raising the bar of performance and increasing the quality of its leadership.

At AB InBev, as at GE, losing a top performer is a sin, and there's a company-wide goal of top performer retention. In a recent case of a top performer leaving Burger King, the employee was amazed at how much people tried to dissuade him from leaving once he announced his decision. He had only recently been put into a "Future Promises" list of high potential employees that were expected to take leadership positions within the company in the near future.

The bonus pool

The bonus pool is the total amount of cash available for distribution at year-end. It's also called the size of the pie, and is a function of the company's Economic Value Added:

Pie = EVA * X%

EVA = Nopat – Cost of Capital

Where:

Nopat = Net Operating Profit After Taxes

Cost of Capital = Invested Capital * WACC

Invested Capital = Operating Assets

WACC = Weighted Average Cost of Capital

To get the potential bonus per employee, which is a factor that multiplies annual salary, we divide the pie by the company's monthly payroll:

Potential Bonus = Pie / Monthly Payroll

We then know that the available bonus is, for instance, four months' salary for each employee; but the actual amount earned is given by the employee's position in the bell curve, as we saw in Figure 7.

Excellence Programs

Employees not eligible for management bonuses take part in the company's various Excellence Programs, which are organized within different regions and divisions. AB InBev took inspiration from Anheuser-Busch on these initiatives, which are basically competitions between factories, sales teams, and distribution centers.

Excellence programs entail a group of usually five collective goals for each unit, which are actively pursued by the teams. As we can grasp from AmBev's 2003 Annual Report:

> *These programs were created to maximize efficiency within different units, that compete with each other for the greatest scores based on the achievement of several goals and procedures. Employees on winning units make extra compensation, and the title of "Ambassadors" if they win the contests for more than three times. Beyond motivating people, excellence programs are the backbone of our cost cutting initiatives.*

A specific example is the Sales Excellence Program. Each sales team competes with its regional peers for the prize, which is calculated as a multiplier of the Profit Sharing Program (a very similar logic to the size of the pie and potential bonus.) AmBev, for example, has cut deals with most of the unions active in the brewing industry so they are able to use this strategy. They pay down to no profit sharing at all to losing units, and pay up to three times the profit sharing amount to winning units.

2

Informality

Talented people like simplicity. That's where they thrive.
　　　　　　　- Carlos Brito, 2012 Endeavor CEO Summit

We also believe in keeping it simple: with decisions based on clear, agreed-upon approaches and common sense. That means constantly rooting out complexity, and streamlining processes that get in the way of decision-making and execution.
　　　　　　　- AB InBev's 2014 Annual Report

The second pillar of the pro-talent work environment is informality, which can be seen in a number of different settings and occasions.

An informal workplace fosters communication and transparency, ensures the approachability of senior executives, and is a backbone of meritocracy, since it makes it difficult for mediocre people to hide behind closed doors and corner offices. Great people also like to wear informal clothes, which impose no false status, and appreciate an environment where the best argument wins, with no attention to rank or seniority, but only to facts and data.

Open floor plans

As Carlos Brito said in his Stanford presentation, "I have no office. I sit with my direct reports at a big bench—my marketing guy on my right, my operations guy at my left, and my finance guy on my back."

There are great advantages to having everyone sit close together with no walls between them. First of all, teams can talk to each other without having to move around the office, which increases information flow and efficiency. Brito has said he constantly holds one- to five-minute meetings with his key aides, changing topics quickly and making decisions without the need to check schedules and physically move to a meeting room with (often) a host of unnecessary people.

Another advantage of open floor plans is that they prevent people from hiding behind doors. Carlos said in the same presentation, "Offices are for mediocre people who like to hide behind their doors and play games, et cetera." As harsh as this statement may sound, it is mostly true. People are in the office to work. Workers who want privacy may leave their tables and look for a quiet place to deal with their personal lives, but that must be the exception, not the rule. When work requires privacy, as in the case of confidential matters, staff can use conference rooms.

Another important pro of open floor plans is what I will call approachability. Open setups enhance constant communication between different hierarchical levels. Corner offices, or just walled offices, impose a kind of respect that is detrimental; it imposes fear and shame on workers if they "interrupt" superiors' privacy. But talking to your boss is not, and should not be seen, as interruption. It is an essential part of a healthy work environment.

Casual dress code

The trio's management informality is enhanced by allowing employees to wear mostly casual clothing to work. It reinforces the value of open floor plans in that it also fosters equality between hierarchical levels. Bosses should not use their position or their clothing to impose respect; they should earn their team's respect through example, performance, and argument.

Carlos Brito is always seen in jeans, with shirts embroidered with logos of AB Inbev's brands. The same outfit serves Marcel and Beto, who are rarely seen in suits, and the brewery's salesmen and executives alike. Jorge Paulo adopted the uniform of khaki pants and short-sleeve shirts in Garantia times, and has never dropped it.

Horizontal organizational structure

Informal companies foster environments where the best argument, not the highest hierarchy, drives decisions. Employees of all levels are welcome to join discussions if they have fact-based, well-rounded opinions that add to the topics at hand. In such an environment, leaders cannot hide beneath their titles, and enjoy the full benefit of having hired and nurtured talent better than themselves.

Simplicity

Common sense is as good as fancy concepts. Simple is better than complicated.

- Garantia's 18 Commandments

The last cornerstone of an informal culture is simplicity, as evident in the very down-to-earth manner with which the trio, and their companies' executives, run their businesses, and conduct their personal lives.

As is evident to anyone who takes the time to watch their keynotes online, the language chosen by Jorge Paulo Lemann, Marcel Telles, and Carlos Brito (those whose talks are most abundant) is incredibly simple and understated. They always refer to employees as "people" and not associates or human capital; they talk about owner mindset, and not empowerment or accountability; and they talk about being great, good or mediocre—very straight to the point.

The language and content of their management principles are also very enlightening: they praise copying what's best instead of trying to reinvent the wheel, as well as hard work and knowing the operations firsthand. These are very old-school, working-class values with which anyone can relate. AB InBev's leaders firmly believe great people can understand matters so thoroughly that they can distill complex concepts into simple, approachable explanations that the whole company can easily grasp.

3

Candor

Transparency and free information flow ease decision-making and minimize conflicts.

- Garantia's 18 Commandments

We believe common sense and simplicity are usually better guidelines than unnecessary sophistication and complexity.

- AB InBev's 10 Principles

In big companies, only good news arrives at the top.

- Carlos Brito, Endeavor CEO Summit

The third and last pillar of an environment where great talent feels at home is a candid one, where people discuss topics openly, with little tolerance for internal politics, hidden agendas, and opacity.

Candor is intimately related to informality, and could even be discussed as one topic. But I choose to stay with Carlos Brito's three pillars for the sake of fidelity to the company's internal understanding of its culture.

According to Brito, a candid environment is one where "everyone in the company can speak up as long as they are respectful and constructive," and where "people know where they stand" in terms of their performance and the company's plans for them[12].

A worker can and must disagree with colleagues and superiors if he or she believes that the topic at

---

[12] From Brito's "View from the Top" talks at Stanford.

hand is being misunderstood or that the plan of action being taken is wrong.

According to Vicente Falconi, encouraging employees to speak up brings them great enthusiasm, since they're able to persuade colleagues and take an active part in the direction taken by the company.

Jack Welch touched the same subject in his 2000 Annual Report at GE:

Informality is not generally seen as a particularly important characteristic in most large institutions, but it is in ours. Informality is more than just being a first-name company; it's not just a sense of managers parading around the factory floor in suits, or of reserved parking spaces or other trappings of rank and status. It's deeper than that. At GE it's an atmosphere in which anyone can deliver a view, an idea, to anyone else, and it will be listened to and valued, regardless of the seniority of any party involved. Leaders today must be equally comfortable making a sales call or sitting in a boardroom: informality is an operating philosophy as well as a cultural characteristic.

Falconi, the consultant, also speaks about the obsession for always seeking the "truth" through facts and data-based discussions, where the best argument must always win, despite seniority levels, years with the company, or other subjective factors that are not related to the "truth" of the matter.

A final aspect of candor is that, according to Brito, "great people like to know where they stand." This relates to two things: first, leaders must always provide reports with open, candid feedback that allows them to improve their weaknesses and enhance their strengths. Second, great people like to know if the company has great plans for them. They like to know they're ripe for a promotion, or that certain steps are between them and a significant career move.

4

Growth

The most competitive companies in the world frequently boast about their "up or out" cultures: employees either move up, as a reward for high performance and a way to clear space for up-and-coming juniors, or leave the company altogether, spit out by the system.

But in order for upward mobility to happen, the top positions of a company (which, because of the pyramid shape of organizations, are usually few) must be frequently recycled. But isn't turnover at the top bad for organizations, causing loss of knowledge and experience (frequently to competitors) and slack?

The answer to this conundrum lies in growth. If we analyze AB InBev's history, the company has grown steadily and sharply since it all started with the Brazil-based Brahma. Since the trio believes their only really sustainable competitive advantage is their management style, they sought to chase growth by purchasing "mature businesses, with pulverized (and/or weak) ownership, strong, recognized brands and poor management," where "external and internal owners could make a difference," in the words of Marcel Telles. Acquisitions supplied top-line growth, and management turnaround supplied earnings growth, a combination that pleased ambitious employees and shareholders alike.

Acquisitions enabled Antarctica—then AmBev and finally InBev—to export talented individuals to a number of M&A-created positions (the Brazilians secretly pride themselves in having "taken over" much of AB InBev's management structure) around the globe. That is the upward mobility that enabled them to compensate armies of great executives with increased authority, responsibility, and promotions, without the much-feared turnover at the top of its ranks.

5

The talent factory

We always nurtured a colossal pipeline of brilliant, ambitious, entrepreneurial people.

- Marcel Telles, Endeavor CEO Summit

We hire people with the potential to be better than we are, ensure that our leaders engage them fully, and challenge them to perform at their best. At the same time, we invest heavily in attracting the best people, developing their potential, and enriching their opportunities through a range of programs and initiatives. We have continued to refine and enhance our talent recruitment, learning and development initiatives to build a pipeline of talent, meet the changing needs of a growing business, and cultivate the next generation of leaders.

                       - AB InBev's 2014 Annual Report

It's hard to know what comes first: a great pool of talent, or sharp growth. But the fact is that growth and talent must walk hand-in-hand, or everything falls apart. Understanding how AB InBev's talent factory works is in great measure an understanding of the core of its management culture, which is so heavily based on people.

The Global Management Trainee program

Young people are idealists by nature. When you try to recruit some older professional, he's already been through a lot, a lot of situations that've made him kind of cynical. He's heard all those promises, but has also seen firsthand that most people say them, but don't practice them.[13]

                       - Marcel Telles, Endeavor CEO Summit

---

[13] Translation by the author.

DREAM, PEOPLE, CULTURE

A trademark of the 3G management style is their quick implementation of comprehensive trainee programs.

Hiring at the base of the pyramid is of the essence. According to Jim Collins, author of *Built to Last: Successful Habits of Visionary Companies*, with whom AB InBev's board of directors consults yearly, hiring at the bottom is a trait of the most successful companies, because it allows thorough cultural indoctrination and minimizes the hiring of people who have been contaminated with other culture's weaknesses.

The most straightforward way to do this is through a comprehensive trainee program (or several, in the case with AB InBev.)

The company holds an annual recruitment process that spans almost six months, beginning with a senior management roadshow to the world's top undergraduate programs (Marcel Telles did these university presentations for a long time; Carlos

Brito does a number of them nowadays, as do other C-level executives), a practice they believe enables them to attract much better talent than their large competitors, who send HR people to do recruiting. According to Marcel Telles at Endeavor's CEO Summit:

> *I would recruit against the large corporate behemoths, head-to-head. The only difference is that [AmBev] sent its owners recruiting, whereas our competitors sent John Doe, from HR[14].*

Candidates are screened through multiple tests and interviews, after which they meet again, now on a more personalized basis, with top executives, who give their final sign-off on the most promising candidates. This ensures culture fit, and tips the scale towards AB InBev if the candidate has competing offers.

---

[14] Translation by the author.

DREAM, PEOPLE, CULTURE

In 2014, AB InBev's Global Management Trainee (GMT) program had a class of 147 young professionals, chosen from a pool of more than 94,000 candidates. It's a massive and quite selective program. According to AmBev's 2014 Annual Report:

> The trainee program was created to develop young talented professionals with an ample, generalist view of the industry and the skills that enable them to undertake key management roles within the company on the short and medium-terms. The recruiting process encompasses seven steps, from the sign-up to on-line quizzes, to a final interview with members of our C-suite. The selected few go through ten months of training. In the first five months, the focus is on acquiring a strategic view of our business, working through manufacturing, sales, and corporate functions. In the second part, they focus on one specific area of the company, after being thoroughly followed by our People Development team[15].

In addition to the GMT program, AmBev also has a specific manufacturing trainee program, focused on developing industrial engineers and brewing masters, for technically-oriented undergrads. Finally, there's an internship program that hires students before their graduation for part-time or summer-vacation positions.

MBAs

AB InBev and the other companies owned by the trio also hire top-tier MBAs. It all started with Carlos Brito, who was the first student to have his MBA financed by Jorge Paulo Lemann, in the 1980s. After his Stanford program ended, Brito was hired at Garantia, and went on to Brahma after the acquisition. Lemann and his two main partners then founded Fundação Estudar, a charity focused on handing out merit-based loans to promising graduate and undergraduate Brazilian students.

---

[15] Translation by the author.

Fundação Estudar gave the trio an unprecedented pipeline of high-quality postgraduate students (since then, the NGO has extended its program to undergrads), a great number of which were hired within the trio's companies.

MBAs from the world's top business schools are selected for summer internships, and the top performers are then extended full-time offers, very much like what happens at Wall Street firms. As the 2014 AB InBev Annual Report explains,

> Our global MBA program draws qualified candidates from such top business schools as Harvard, Stanford, Chicago-Booth, MIT Sloan, Columbia, Wharton and Kellogg in the U.S., as well as London Business School and IESE in Europe and CEIBS in Hong Kong. In 2014, we selected 21 MBAs for the program from a pool of 642 applicants.

Promotions and "people chess"

With the base of the pyramid thoroughly supplied by internships, trainee programs, and MBA hires, the company goes on to nurture the talent funnel all the way to the top, through promotions, formal training, strategic career moves, and fast-tracks for the most promising.

Training, as we'll see further down the road, is widespread through AB InBev; that started its corporate university program in the 1990s with the founding of Brahma University.

AB InBev is very strategic in how it handles promotions. As mentioned previously, every year leaders are required to name two possible successors who have (or are going to have in the near future) the suitable skills to take on their roles should they be promoted (or leave the company.) These promotions are discussed, at least at AmBev, in a "People Chess" meeting, where the company's leaders, alongside the People and Management

Department, discuss who's being promoted, and to which functions.

The company strongly encourages lateral moves that take people out of their comfort zones. According to Brito's View from the Top talk:

> *We like taking people out of their comfort zones. We do a lot of that; and it's been working fine. We get someone who's been at a position for three, four years, for example in finance, and suddenly throw him into sales.*

> *We've learned that people only grow when taken out of their comfort zones, in the same way that companies only grow when taken out of their comfort zones. The company only grows when its people grow.*

These moves are all decided in these People Chess meetings, where management discusses how future promotions can enhance employee skills. Replacement costs are minimized, since there's always someone ready to take on the newly-opened position.

People bets

Another important tool are "People Bets." People bets are high-potential employees chosen for their exceptional performance and culture fit, who are informally stamped as "bets," and thus given more intense love and care in the form of growth opportunities and training.

People Bets were initially called "high-potentials," but the company learned that some people became entitled and lost some of their motivation to keep working hard. Retention of People Bets is a company-wide goal.

PART 2: DREAM

FRANCISCO S. HOMEM DE MELLO

6

A big dream

The greater danger for most of us lies not in setting our aim too high and falling short; but in setting our aim too low, and achieving our mark.

- Michelangelo

A big and challenging dream makes everyone row in the same direction.

- Garantia's 18 Commandments

Our shared dream energizes everyone to work in the same direction. To be the Best Beer Company Bringing People Together for a Better World.

- AB InBev's 10 Principles

Jorge Paulo Lemann, Marcel Telles, Beto Sicupira, and their executives talk tirelessly about dreaming big: "always dream big. Big dreams and small dreams take the same effort," Lemann says.

But what does that mean?

Dreaming big means aiming for a big, ambitious goal. This goal is constantly mentioned within their companies' hallways as a mantra. Much more approachable and objective than having missions and visions.

Variable compensation and stock ownership are powerful tools in aligning and motivating employees, offering them a real chance at improving their lives meaningfully. But they aren't enough.

At Garantia, money wasn't a problem. Several former partners of the investment bank are notoriously rich, in part because of the incredibly high bonuses they made at the firm. There are stories of ex-partners buying helicopters, sports cars, and luxury properties days after getting their year-end rewards. But according to Cristiane Correa, author of *Dream Big*, the trio was frustrated with their employees' lack of commitment to a life of hard work and purpose. This is made evident by the fact that few of Garantia's partners ever took part at the trio's other businesses.

Daniel Pink, the American author of *Drive*, is one of the advocates of alternative motivating factors, such as a sense of purpose (working for "something bigger") and autonomy (working independently towards a goal), apart from the common-place reward/punishment system controlled by our brain's frontal cortexes.

The theme is also explored by Jim Collins, who coined the term Big, Hairy, Audacious Goals (BHAG), to suggest that companies that inspire their employees with a great, challenging goal, are the ones that succeed in the long run.

With these lessons, the trio understood it had to attract people who are motivated by more than money: a big dream. With that in mind, Marcel Telles established Brahma's first ever big dream: to become Brazil's largest and best brewing company.

When Antarctica was acquired, and the first big dream conquered, they aimed their cross-hairs at Latin American domination, and set out on an aggressive expansion through greenfield operations and acquisitions.

After the Interbrew deal, the trio went on to dream of dominating the world's beer market, which became a reality with the purchase of Anheuser-Busch in 2008. It's hard to say what comes next. Some people say Pepsi, or even Coca-Cola, are their secret dreams, something that's become increasingly realistic after their successful partnership with Warren Buffet on the Heinz deal.

FRANCISCO S. HOMEM DE MELLO

7

From dreams to goals

Dreaming big is not limited to board-room discussions, strategic planning, or endomarketing. It is the basis of the company's complete goals-based management system, developed with Vicente Falconi in the 1990s.

From the "big dream," which is the company's long-term business goal, achievable in three to five years, the company breaks down its yearly plan, and then the goals and tasks of every employee, from the CEO to the plants' janitorial staff.

The system is very well summarized by a diagram created by Vicente Falconi, in his *True Power* book, and filled in with very simplistic hypothetical examples by the author:

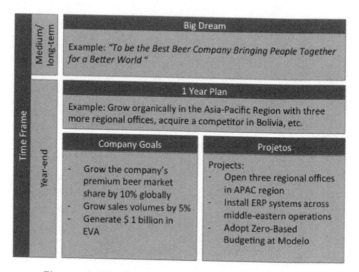

Figure 8: Big dreams break down into goals.
Source: Vicente Falconi, AB InBev, author.

This way, the company generates an actual framework with which to make everybody "row in the same direction." From the big dream, the company breaks down company-wide yearly goals, and then CEO goals, VP goals, Director goals, all the way down to the factory employees, who are all aligned by targets derived from the company's Big Dream.

Breaking goals down

A systematic goals breakdown system was probably one of Vicente Falconi's main contributions to the trio's management style, as can be seen in the following chart:

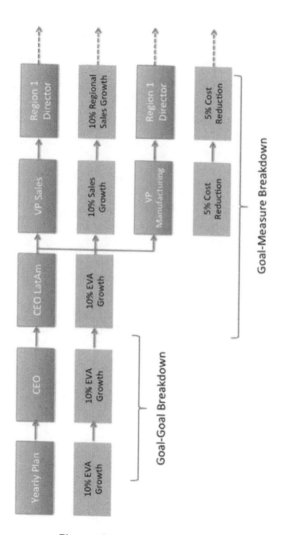

Figure 9: Goals breakdown
Source: Vicente Falconi, author.

Type A Breakdown: Goal-Measure

Some goals can be broken down in measures. If goals can't be broken down in measures, it's because the goal is an action to be taken.

Measures are the components that lead to achieving a goal. For example, in order to achieve higher EBITDA, a company must increase sales, and/or reduce costs, and/or reduce expenses, and/or increase productivity. These are measures.

When a goal is broken down in measures, these measures must themselves become someone else's goals (when they're added to a time-frame.) So the CEO's EBITDA goal is broken down to a sales measure, which then becomes the goal of the VP Sales.

A goal-goal breakdown is called a Type A breakdown by Vicente Falconi, and looks like this:

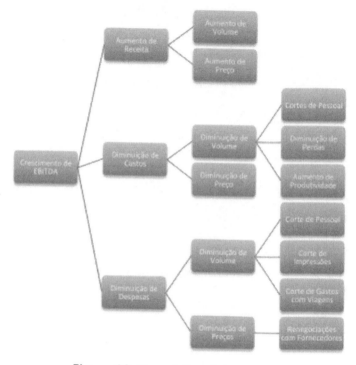

Figure 10: Type A Breakdown.

Type B Breakdown: Goal-Goal

Sometimes, goals can't be broken down, because they've become someone's actions, but they can be passed down to employees who share the same goal. That's the case, for example, with sales increases, all the way from the Global VP Sales to a Sales rep based in New York City or São Paulo:

they can share the same goal, albeit having subsequently smaller scopes in their regional coverage.

FRANCISCO S. HOMEM DE MELLO

8

Gaps and method

Gaps are the difference between reality and goals.
Gaps can also be called "problems."

Gaps can be of two main kinds:

1   Improvement gaps
Improvement gaps open up when the company
needs a qualitative or quantitative performance

leap. Using last chapter's example, growing EBITDA by 10% is an improvement gap.

2   Maintenance gaps

A maintenance gap happens when some key-performance indicator is lagging behind its predetermined standard. Let's say a certain factory worker has a goal of maintaining an error level of less than one problem per thousand units bottled. If his error level goes to two units per thousand, he then has an improvement goal to get back on track.

How should gaps be closed?

A company reaches goals by closing gaps. How to do that is one of Professor Falconi's contributions to the trio's management style. Falconi calls it the "method," a word that was inspired by the late 17th century's Renaissance, when the "scientific method" was created. It's defined by the Oxford dictionary as "systematic observation, measurement, and experimentation, and in the formulation, test, and change of hypotheses."

In a more practical manner, the scientific method can be described as a framework for problem solving. The tool for closing gaps is the PDCA cycle, which stands for Plan-Do-Check-Act:

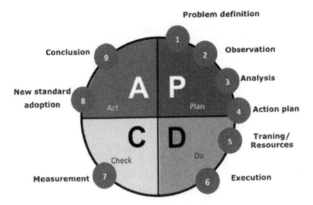

Figure 11: PDCA cycle
Source: Vicente Falconi, author.

If we look closely at the PDCA cycle and its application for closing gaps, we can plot these cycles on a graph that looks like this:

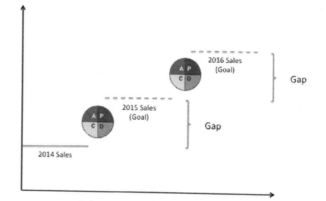

Figure 12-a: PDCA application in improvement gaps.

When the PDCA cycle is used for maintenance gaps, it's called SDCA, and looks like this on the graph:

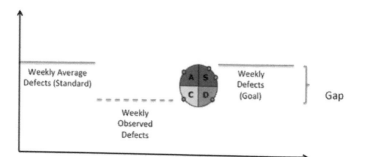

Figure 13-b: SDCA application in maintenance gaps.

A gap example

A scientist starts by defining a problem to be solved (or theory to be proved.) For example, someone at AB InBev may be interested in understanding why sales fell by 10% in a certain Los Angeles neighborhood.

The employee formulates a hypothesis as to why the problem (the sales drop) happened. For example, he may conjecture that it happened because of a major political demonstration that happened in the region.

The next step is observing the problem in action, and analyzing possible causes. There are two main tools used in PDCA analysis: the Five Whys and the Fishbone Graph.

Five Whys

The Five Whys are a method to get to the root cause of a problem. When people stay at the first layer of a problem (the first "why") they tend to overlook the real root cause. Therefore, the tool is to ask Why five subsequent times (or as many times as needed) until the final root cause of a problem is found.

In our example:

Q: Sales fell by 10%. Why?

A: Because of the demonstration.

Q: Why the demonstration affected sales?

A: Because some streets were closed, and our trucks couldn't reach merchants.

Q: Why didn't we use smaller trucks to deliver goods on that day?

A: Because we don't own them.

There! You've reached the root cause of the sales drop, which is much more subtle and specific than merely blaming the demonstrations.

The root cause often makes an action plan to solve the problem obvious. In this case, the suggestion is to buy a smaller truck for use during the demonstrations scheduled for the next month. If sales are maintained after the experiment, the company then adopts a new standard: having smaller trucks for those events.

The fishbone graph

The fishbone graph (also called an Ishikawa Diagram, or Cause-and-Effect diagram) is nothing more than a way to plot possible causes after the Five Whys reasoning, to clear up the thought process of all the involved parties. Let's plot our example in a fishbone graph:

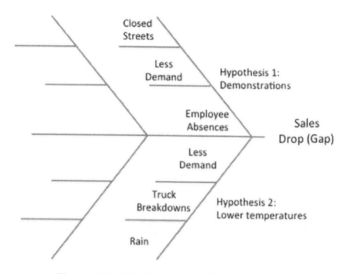

Figure 14: Fishbone graph application
Source: Vicente Falconi, author.

Advanced tools

The Five Whys and the fishbone graph are basic analysis tools that work for the great majority of the problems faced by companies worldwide.

When companies are in a very advanced stage of method adoption, they may need to adopt more sophisticated tools of analysis, like statistical software such as Excel (basic) and MatLab (advanced).

These analyses are the responsibility of internal consulting professionals, trained in the ways of Six Sigma (a variation of Total Quality) and graded for their level of expertise like Japanese martial arts practitioners, from white belts all the way to black belts, across the organization.

These professionals analyze problems and formulate action plans for a living.

The importance of gaps

Gaps are a recurring theme within AB InBev, which closely observes the difference between where the company and its executives are today, and where they want to be in the future (which is then broken down as goals to the whole company.)

The idea of a Big, Hairy, Audacious Goal, according to Collins, is to unite people around a common, greater goal, and also to get them to "stretch" their capabilities—to go beyond what they believed could be done.

According to Carlos Brito, "A dream makes us tick much more than missions and visions. Missions are for the military, and visions are for...I don't know what visions are for."

According to Falconi, goals are how a company achieves its dreams, and they have to stretch people's skills. The magical figure, according to him, is that 80% of an employee's goal/gap (or the company's, for that matter) has to be achievable with the skills presently owned by him. The other 20% are the stretch that makes the employee go the extra mile[16]. Brito summarizes the concept: "A dream has to be sufficiently stretched so that you know 80% how to get there; you have to learn the other 20% as you go."

---

[16] Excuse me for the cliché.

Gaps and stretches also take employees out of their comfort zones and create a healthy amount of pressure. Brito believes that AB InBev attracts people who work best under pressure—a culture that's not for everybody: "Human beings are rational, and optimize for their energy expenditures, doing just what is enough to clear hurdles. That is the importance of raising the bar."

FRANCISCO S. HOMEM DE MELLO

PART 3:
CULTURE

9

Ownership mindset

Everything has to have an owner with authority and accountability. Debating is good, but in the end, someone has to decide.

- Garantia's 18 Commandments

We are a company of owners. Owners take results personally.
We are never completely satisfied with our results, which are the fuel of our company. Focus and zero complacency guarantee lasting competitive advantage.

- AB InBev's 10 Principles

An owner's mindset is something that's expected from every employee of the trio's companies, and which makes all the difference, from the simplest menial daily problems, like cleanliness at the factory floor, to the strategic direction of the company. Owners think long-term, have a deep commitment to the company's success, are naturally accountable for their choices and actions, and so on.

References to an ownership mentality are ample in the company's website, business principles, Annual Reports, and keynote speeches given by the trio and its main executives, as we can see in AB InBev's 2014 Annual Report:

In our culture, team members think and act like owners: they take results personally; are accountable for their actions; make decisions in the long-term best interests of the business; and execute with focus, excellence, and integrity. This ownership mentality is reinforced by setting stretched but achievable targets, and ensuring that all team members understand their roles in meeting those targets. Incentive programs give senior leaders and other top performers the opportunity to reinvest their bonus in our shares, with a company match. But our ownership culture goes beyond owning shares—it is about owning responsibility for our commitments to consumers, for the creation of shareholder value, and for delivering on our Dream.

A good system of goals breakdown, backed by de facto variable compensation, is the first pillar of an ownership culture: employees really feel their lives change for the better if they truly contribute to the success of the company, which is, in turn, the success of its shareholders.

But variable compensation is not enough, as we can conclude after digesting the results of gigantic bonuses in most Wall Street firm's cultures. Both Lehman Brothers and Bear Stearns had huge variable compensation systems in place. But incentives were not aligned, i.e., executives didn't think like owners.

On the other hand, most Fortune 500 companies have some sort of stock options program (where employees have the option, but not the obligation, of buying company shares at a future date, at a pre-determined price.) These programs should align executives and stockholders, right? But they don't. Since a great number of Fortune 500 companies have lackluster performances, and the overall U.S. stock market's headwinds haven't really helped, executives tend to view these programs as a low probability of making them any money. There's no downside to the executive, as there is, clearly, to the stockholder. How's that conundrum fixed?

The partnership model: beyond stock options and bonuses

Beyond variable compensation, the best performing employees, that truly incorporate AmBev's culture,

DREAM, PEOPLE, CULTURE

and have a history of long-term commitment to the company, have access to a stock ownership plan. This plan enables them to purchase company stock at a 10% discount from the market price, and require them to hold the stock for a minimum of five years.

- AmBev's 2003 Annual Report

As we can see from the quote above, top performing, committed executives (around 700 of them, from more than 100,000 employees globally) are invited to purchase stock at a 10% discount to trading market prices, a model inspired by Garantia, and consequently Goldman Sachs.

While the employee is given the option to buy into stock, he is actually required to use cash to buy them (and can be financed by the company). Stock-options plans, on the other hand, don't require the actual purchase of stock for cash until the vesting period has ended, and the stock can be immediately sold, with no parked cash whatsoever. "We don't want employees trading their stock options to exploit some short-term market opportunity, so we require a minimum vesting period before which converted stock can be sold," said Marcel, in an interview to HSM Magazine.

In the partnership model, employees actually win and lose money just like their bosses, the shareholders (which they have, in fact, become). They can use bonuses to pay down financing and buy up stock, tying a relevant portion of their personal net worth to the company's shares.

Accountability

Another important aspect of ownership mentality is accountability: everything, throughout the company, has to have an owner: someone clearly responsible for the outcomes of a process, decision, or project.

There are a number of corporate cultures that encourage groupthink and committees, and enable a lack of clear responsibilities. At AB InBev, it's the exact opposite.

One interesting example of how the ownership mentality translates into a very commonplace process within the company is budgeting. The trio's companies all practice Zero-Based Budgeting (ZBB), a technique we'll go over in greater detail in the next part of the book.

In a ZBB matrix, each cost center, or expense center, has an owner: People and Management Department has a budget owner. Finance has one, as do Sales, Supply Chain, and so on. The owner is accountable for their team's budget and expenses, and for making sure both go hand-in-hand.

On the matrix are all the different expense items a budget entails, such as office supplies, traveling expenses, payroll, insurance, health benefits, etc. The interesting thing is that every one of these lines, called expense "packages," *also* has an owner within the organization, who is responsible for knowing them from the inside-out, negotiating better deals, and making sure the overall package budget of the company isn't exceeded. It brings an important secondary level of ownership to the budgeting process, which helps ensure expenses are always controlled, and possibly reduced. Needless to say, package owners (and business-unit budget owners) have goals tied to their results.

In $ Millions	Unit Owner	VP	VP	COO	Total
Package Owner	Package / Unit	People/Mgmt	Sales	Supply-Chain	Package Total
People Manager	Payroll	50	300	150	500
Sourcing Manager	Supply Chain	5	45	10	60
Supply Chain Direct	Trips	1	25	20	46
Treasury Manager	Consultancies	3	5	5	13
Finance Analyst	Insurance	0	5	10	15
	Unit Total	59	380	195	

Figure 14: ZBB Matrix

Figure 15: ZBB Matrix.

The advantages of having an army of owners

Ownership mentality is very actively sought in the trio's companies, from the GMT recruiting process all the way up to the partnership program we've discussed. As we've said, owners produce more and better work. That's why senior management dedicate a lot of time to vetting junior candidates, ensuring they think long-term, have a hands-on work ethic, and are deeply committed to great results.

First, owners are committed to businesses for the long term, and therefore think long term. As Carlos Brito likes to joke, "People treat their cars much better than they treat rentals"—because they are stuck with their cars and face the consequence of their actions. In other words, owners are the ones who live and die for their businesses.

Long-term thinking can be enforced by issuing stock options that have very strict monetization guidelines. "We don't want employees trading their stock options to exploit some short-term market opportunity, so we require a minimum vesting period before which converted stock can be sold," said Marcel, in an interview to HSM Magazine, a Brazilian publication. Employees also note that there's an unwritten expectation that they carry as much company stock as possible, though it is acceptable to sell stock to buy a (reasonably priced) apartment, or for other infrequent expenses and investments, such as marriage and kids.

Second, the trio views a hands-on attitude as a fundamental attribute of great people. As Carlos Brito said at Stanford, "In school, you have to deal with your finals, no matter what happens. You can ask for help, but ultimately, it's you who has to sit down and write your test. The same goes for sports: if your team is losing the game, you are going to try to change the strategy or do something."

Corporations, on the other hand, are vulnerable to a disease in which people don't care enough to solve problems they face; they leave the responsibility to the company. According to Brito,

When you go into the corporate world, all of a sudden there's this image of or idea or perception that there is something of a higher hierarchy that is the company. And so you have a problem and you say, 'Yeah, I'm

sure the company will come up with something. They'll tell us what to do. Maybe they will think of something.

But companies are built on the sum of the collective actions of all employees, so the 3G likes people who tackle problems with their bare hands and look for ways to solve them.

To enforce this kind of hands-on attitude, the company has to give authority and autonomy to employees to chase solutions to their problems— obviously, within parameters related to their functions and seniority levels—and hold them accountable for these decisions, ensuring that the company learns with the outcomes.

This relates to the Toyota Production System, where employees are encouraged to supply improvement ideas to their leaders in a never-ending process. Autonomy, as Daniel Pink, author of *Drive: The Surprising Truth about What Motivates Us*, is a major motivator of people.

FRANCISCO S. HOMEM DE MELLO

10

Benchmarking

Common sense is as good as fancy concepts. Simple is better than complicated.
Innovations that add value are useful, but copying practices that already work is usually easier.

- Garantia's 18 Commandments

A big trait of the trio's 3G management style is adopting the world's best practices, when available, and then improving upon them, instead of trying to reinvent the wheel at great cost of time and money. I've tried to make this crystal clear throughout the book by referencing quotes from Jack Welch's GE annual reports, Goldman Sachs business principles, and Walmart's Sam Walton's autobiography, which are, openly, the 3G's greatest inspirations, as well as The Toyota Way, which serves as a very significant backbone for everything Professor Falconi implemented at Brahma, AmBev, InBev, and AB InBev.

The trio is very humble when speaking about their culture. Maybe too humble. But it gives us a bird's eye view into how the culture came into being. In the words of Jorge Paulo Lemann, in an interview to Brazilian HSM Management:

Amongst our greatest influences are Goldman Sachs, probably the world's best investment bank — with them, we learned meritocracy, intense employee training, and the need to give people constant growth opportunities. With Walmart's founder, Sam Walton, [whom Lemann and his partners visited when they acquired Lojas Americanas, as a result of a cold letter sent to the world's top retailers asking for "help"] we've learned that we could reach the pot of gold at the end of the rainbow with patience and perseverance, and no shortcuts, as well as motivating employees, and treating them, as well as clients, well. Finally, with GE, we'd read everything about Jack Welch. GE's annual reports were our Bible. Based on these three streams, and what we'd learned with our businesses [Garantia, Lojas Americanas, etc.], we went on to build our own culture.

The trio visited Goldman Sachs in the Garantia days. Walmart was visited when they were learning the ropes of the retail business at Lojas Americanas. It's widely unknown that they also visited Anheuser-Busch when they purchased Brahma, which shows the amount of admiration, and then fierceness, that led them to acquire the company. Magim Rodriguez, former CEO of AmBev, is quoted as saying,

Benchmarking is something that works in any industry. Back at AmBev, Marcel and I traveled the world looking for references. We visited Anheuser-Busch, Coors, and at least half a dozen other breweries in trying to learn their best practices.

11

Focus

Focus is of the essence. It's impossible to be excellent at everything, so concentrate on the few things that really matter.

- Garantia's 18 Commandments

Focus is probably one of the most misused management terms. Almost every company refers to client focus, or focus on results, but it's truly a driving force in the day-to-day activities of the 3G companies.

Focus can be translated into many forms.

Customer focus

Putting the consumer at the center of all we do is a key element of our culture. To do that, we focus on delivering great brands, making products of impeccable quality, and providing a superior experience in a responsible way. We respect the heritage of the brewer's craft, while using the latest technologies and media to connect with consumers.

- AB InBev's 2014 Annual Report

The consumer is the Boss. We serve our consumers by offering brand experiences that play a meaningful role in their lives, and always in a responsible way.

- AB InBev's 10 Principles

Like other large, successful consumer brands, such as P&G and Unilever, AB InBev strives to be at the forefront of product innovations that anticipate customer's varying habits and trends. There's an interesting anecdote that depicts how learning to be customer centric came the hard way.

When Brahma decided to expand into Argentina, back in the 1990s, it sent a bunch of young executives to the nearby country in one of the company's first forays abroad. The company opted to bottle its beers in a 0.6L vessel that was commonplace then in the Brazilian market. But Argentinians, as well as Uruguayans, didn't use 0.6L bottles. They were used to 1L bottles, as tall as the smaller ones, but fatter, carrying almost 50% more beer. It was a fiasco: people treated them like a giant long-neck bottle, drinking them by the bottle.

That was a long time ago. Nowadays, the company is truly customer centric, leading the market in innovative mixes and presentations throughout the world. In AB InBev's 2014 Annual Report, the company describes its newly-created Growth Driven Platforms strategy:

People get together in different ways, at different times, and for different reasons. To share special experiences.

FRANCISCO S. HOMEM DE MELLO

To enjoy the pleasures of a great meal. To cheer on their team or listen to their favorite brand. To unwind after a long day. To open their home to friends and family.

We believe our growth depends on understanding what brings people together – and how we can make their occasions even better. To do that, we increasingly seek relevant insights into the population of potential consumers, the preferences of those most likely to favor our brands, the reasons why they get together, and the experiences they value.

Based on these insights, we have created a framework of Growth Driven Platforms, or GDPs, which represent the major occasions for purchasing and consuming our products. We are aligning our marketing, sales, product development and other brand-building activities with the GDPs to ensure that we provide quality products – and brew good times and great experiences – for all the ways people get together.

That's how the company introduced innovations like the family-sized Fusion presentation, which enables Brazilian youngsters to buy the caffeine-infused soda in large amounts for parties at home, or the new MixxTail mojitos and Bud Light Ritas (from marg*eritas*) targeted at non-beer-drinking customers.

Strategic x non-strategic costs

Customer focus takes shape in another interesting way in AB InBev, as best described by the company's 2014 Annual Report:

We aim to convert 'non-working money' into 'working money'—reducing expenditures for ancillary items while investing in brands, marketing, sales efforts, trade programs and other factors that drive top-line and bottom-line growth.

The practice of shaving costs and expenses and out-spending competitors in activities like product R&D, marketing, and branding, was inspired by a little-known book that has been repeatedly distributed by the trio amongst their executives over the years: *Double Your Profits: In Six Months or Less*, by Bob Fifer.

Non-strategic costs and expenses are those that do not directly contribute to the firm's top or bottom line: office materials, middle management overhead, travel expenses, meals, and so on. They should be ruthlessly cut, because, in the words of a former AB InBev executive, "costs grow like nails."

Strategic costs and expenses, on the other hand, are those that may add to the company's top and bottom lines. Advertising, branding, trade marketing, R&D, are all examples of strategic costs and expenses (depending on how the company accounts for them, they can be costs or expenses.) According to Fifer, great companies underspend their competitors on non-strategic costs, and overspend them on strategic ones.

12

Leadership

Leadership by personal example is at the core of our culture. We do what we say.
We will be judged by the quality of our teams.

- AB InBev's 10 Principles

According to Carlos Brito, leaders are those who "need a team in order to reach goals." This definition inspired the dream-people-culture triad, when Marcel Telles and Vicente Falconi defined leaders as "those who reach goals [dream], with their teams [people], in the right way [culture]."

Reaching goals, or making the numbers, is an absolute at AB InBev, and is measured monthly in numbers meetings across the whole company, from top to bottom. But it's very important that goals be reached in teams, which leverage individual performance, within the culture and values of the company. Vicente Falconi summarizes the leader's agenda in an interesting graph, from his *True Power*.

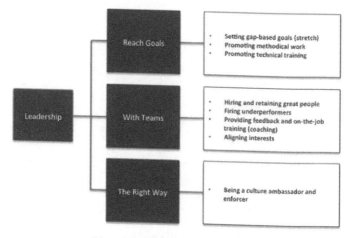

Figure 16: Leader's Agenda
Source: Vicente Falconi.

According to the company's 2014 Annual Report,

Our leaders are expected to set a strong personal example for the company. They must deliver results, live up to their commitments and inspire their teams to do the same. Leaders never take the easy way out, nor do things in a manner that places their own interests above those of the company, consumers, shareholders, employees, and community.

Culture fit and teamwork are both the subject of an annual company-wide 360-degree review, separate from the annual bonus-focused performance review, where leaders are reviewed by subordinates, peers, and bosses, on the ten management principles that are the backbone of AB InBev's culture.

Training

As company principles mandate, a leader's role is to recruit people that are better than him- or herself, and then train, challenge, and retain them.

So challenging and training people, two activities that have to walk hand-in-hand, are a constant concern to the trio's companies.

Challenging people, as we've seen, takes them out of their comfort zones. But that would be reckless if it wasn't followed closely by having successors in place for each position, as well as training the challenged employees with the required skills of their new positions.

Formal training programs date all the way back to 1995, when Brahma founded its Brahma University, and launched its first corporate MBA program, jokingly dubbed internally as the Master in Brahma Administration. Back then, training was also performed by Instituto Brahma, a corporate charity that was later incorporated by the firm's AmBev University. Currently in Brazil, AmBev's corporate MBA is accredited by the Education Ministry, and performed in joint ventures with some of the country's top business schools.

Brahma University became AmBev University, a behemoth that by 2012 had given more than 68,000 courses (both on-line and off-line), with an R$32 million budget (approximately $10 million), distributed in 1500 different programs. Originally, the programs were distributed in five main themes: operational excellence, culture, leadership, management, and marketing. Later, with the Anheuser–Busch acquisition, the trainings were unified under AB InBev University, and the courses were streamlined into three main pillars:

- Functional training, which teaches employees the skills they need to perform their current functions.

- Culture and Leadership, which prepares employees for leadership roles, and infuses them with the cultural values of the company.

- Method, which trains employees in problem-solving (or gap-closing) skills, such as the

Five Whys, and statistical tools. Students are awarded white, green, and black belts.

The company also promotes yearly "best practices" conventions. Applications are gathered throughout the year and reviewed by a team of executives, who rank them and hand out prizes to the best projects. Winners go on to present those practices all across the world at zone-specific conventions, sharing these new benchmarks quickly and effectively across the company. Employees are encouraged to participate in the program.

PART 4:
OPERATIONS

FRANCISCO S. HOMEM DE MELLO

13

Efficiency

Beyond his goals-based management system, which breaks the big dream all the way down to individual employee goals and routine, Vicente Falconi also contributed a lot to AB InBev's manufacturing practices, with roots dating all the way back to Brahma.

It all started in 1991. In the midst of a number of ill-fated economic plans that tried to tame Brazil's whopping (hyper)inflation, Marcel Telles went to Brasilia, the country's administrative capital, to try to persuade the government's industry regulators to let him raise Brahma's prices, which were artificially frozen. Speaking at a Falconi Consultores de Resultado (Falconi's consultancy) event, Marcel recalls,

> *In the 90s, I needed to ask the Ministry of Industry and Commerce for a price raise. That's how I met then secretary Dorothea Weneck. She turned to me and said 'Marcel, do you know Total Quality?' I said 'Yes…' [implying that he answered reluctantly]. She was nice about it, and suggested I go meet professor Vicente Falconi.*

> *Off I went to Minas Gerais after him, and that's how we started our partnership. We needed processes to back up our culture. The president of a country, or a company, they're on the driving seat, and say 'Step on*

the gas, turn right, turn left.' But none of that is really connected to the company's inner workings. For it all to happen, there's got to be a system of goals breakdown.

A lot of that came with Falconi. We coupled his system with our management style. Falconi was an efficiency and management evangelist in Brazil. To us, he was fundamental. It's one thing to manage 250 people, as was the case with Garantia. Another is to manage Brahma and AmBev, where, to be honest, if there are no processes in place, if there's no goals breakdown, nothing happens.

Dorothea Weneck thought TQM-based practices could help Brahma increase its productivity, and compensate for being unable to raise prices.

Telles went to Belo Horizonte, to the university engineering school where Falconi was teaching. Falconi had an undergraduate degree in engineering from UFMG, and a Ph.D. from the Colorado School of Mines. Falconi researched various tools and frameworks derived from the school of

management, which was inspired by the work of
W. Edward Demmings and then developed by
Toyota's Taiichi Ohno, Shingeo Shingo, and Eiji
Toyoda.

Toyota faced a bitter problem. The mass
production system created by Henry Ford worked
very well for the gigantic volume of the American
market. But post-war Japan was a much smaller
market, and couldn't absorb the enormous batches
for which mass production was created. Japanese
consumers loved customizations and variety,
leaving local automakers with no option but to try
to extract the maximum productivity possible from
smaller batches, downsized to its smaller market.

Falconi studied those concepts closely, and brought
a number of them back to Brazil, developing a
complete management style with many traits of
The Toyota Way. His work was translated to
English, and is highly recommended for

businessman and managers alike (just search for Vicente Falconi on Amazon).

"Projeto Manufatura"

In the 1990s, Brahma opened up a brand new plant in Rio de Janeiro called Nova Rio. The factory cost more than $300 million, and was designed to supply beer to the Rio market. At the time, the Rio market was sourced from the São Paulo factories, 300km away, and transportation was making the beer more expensive.

But despite its huge capacity and state-of-the-art technology, Nova Rio was reaching less than 60% of its productive potential (20 million hectoliters), and management couldn't figure out why. Carlos Brito set out to analyze the problem under Professor Falconi's supervision. The result was Projeto Manufatura ('Manufacturing Project'), a comprehensive set of production standards, best practices, and standardized process and routines that became the framework for every AmBev factory, and was afterwards rolled out to InBev and AB InBev. The project, which inspired Falconi's *Daily Work Routine Management* book, achieved the intended results, as AmBev's 2003 Annual Report explained:

In order to improve the efficiency of our manufacturing processes, AmBev implemented the Projeto Manufatura, that's developed standardized policies and procedures for our production lines. The project is based in four pillars: people, management, maintenance, and quality, and was rolled out to all our factories in 2003. The project not only improved factory productivity, but has also considerably reduced fixed costs. This advancement can be seen by the evolution of our maintenance costs (including parts and services) that were reduced by 4% in real terms in 2003.

Several practices adopted by Projeto Manufatura were inspired by the Toyota Production System; others were inspired by Demmings's Total Quality management system. Some examples are the 5Ss, the TPM, and the CQCs (circles of quality control).

FRANCISCO S. HOMEM DE MELLO

14

Costs and budgeting

We manage our costs tightly, to free up resources that will support sustainable and profitable top line growth.

- AB InBev's 10 principles

Being paranoid about costs and expenses—the only variables under our control—helps ensure long-term survival.

- Garantia's 18 Commandments

One of Bob Fifer's greatest insights in *Double Your Profits: In Six Months or Less* is his distinction between strategic and non-strategic costs and expenses, introduced in the chapter where we discussed customer focus.

According to Fifer, strategic costs are those that "clearly bring in business and improve the bottom line." Great examples are advertising, consultancy projects focused on top line growth or bottom line improvement, sales commissions, branding, and R&D.

Non-strategic costs, by exclusion, are those "dead" costs that do not directly bring in business or help the bottom line. Middle management overhead, travel expenses, office supplies, unnecessary fixed assets, personal assistants, etc.

Great businesses have to ruthlessly cut non-strategic costs, and even underspend their competition, while overspending in strategic costs. What we'll discuss next are tools that've enabled AB InBev to trim non-strategic costs to the bare bone.

Page 168

Zero-base budgeting

AmBev uses a budgeting system called Zero-Base Budgeting (ZBB), that stimulates our firm's commitment to cost and expense controls by unpairing current year's budgets to past years' realized numbers. Internally, each business unit and team is responsible for its own budget, and each cost center [and spending package] has its 'owner.'

— AmBev's 2011 Annual Report

The most powerful cost-trimming tool used by AB InBev is Zero-Base Budgeting, with its sister initiative, Zero-Base Costs. This method was developed in the 1970s by an academic named Peter Pyhrr, and made public through a Harvard Business Review article. It broke away from the then established budgeting framework of basing budgets on past years' realized expenses.

In traditional budgeting, executives are called into the process only to justify proposed increments to past year's numbers. If some department had a $15,000 travel budget, its manager is called in to say why he's now proposing $16,000, without being held accountable for why the original number was there in the first place. According to *The Economist*,

> *The percentage [change] would be determined more or less arbitrarily, although it would probably be related in some indeterminate way to the rate of inflation, the company's overall strategy, and the manager's frame of mind that day. ... It encourages managers to focus on the cost increase from year to year rather than on the underlying costs themselves.*

In Phyrr's ZBB, managers have to justify their whole budgets from the ground up every single year. It forces the whole company to reevaluate its needs and discuss everything from the ground up in a cathartic yearly ritual that invariably uncovers inefficiencies.

Benefits are clear: the company develops a thorough understanding of its complete cost and expense structure. At AB InBev, it is extremely hard to come by a budget increase in any expense line without a very serious reason. Holding

Page 170

expenses constant (on the worst case scenarios), and possibly reducing them, yearly, produces incredibly powerful compound effects when sales grow at a level reasonably above inflation. That's where the very significant long-term margin expansion observed in the trio's companies comes from.

Vicente Falconi also applied ZBB to the Minas Gerais government, which was able to reduce its budgetary deficit by more than R$2 billion during Governor Aécio Neves' term.

Shared services center

After the Antarctica acquisition and the formation of AmBev, the company opened its first shared services center (CSC) in Jaguariúna, in the state of São Paulo. According to the company's 2001 annual report, the CSC was built aiming to rationalize operational and administrative (non-strategic) routines, enabling significant economies of scale, productivity gains, and easier adoption of new systems and technologies, such as its Enterprise Resource Planning (ERP) software.

The CSC provided a central location for several back-office activities previously scattered across the company's multiple factories, rep offices, and distribution centers, like payroll, accounts payable, accounts receivable, and so on. It adopted SAP's end-to-end methodology, and the famous ERP system was also simultaneously adopted by the firm.

In end-to-end processes like OTC (Order to Cash), HR (Hire to Retire), and PTP (Procure to Pay), teams and people are divided by processes, not by single-activity silos. A single leader is responsible for the whole process, and can then agree to service levels and internal customer's needs.

Purchasing

AB InBev has centralized purchasing structures for its strategic and non-strategic costs.

Purchases are first scattered across a Pareto distribution: 10% of the purchased items are responsible, in general, for around 70% of the purchasing dollar value. These purchases are handled by the central management team, and frequently involve complex sourcing arrangements and hedging contracts. They are given significant attention.

The other 90% of purchases are responsible for 30% of the purchasing dollar value, and are handled by special purchasing teams that work hand-in-hand with engineering teams, helping them figure out innovative sourcing solutions for services, parts, and other smaller line items.

FRANCISCO S. HOMEM DE MELLO

15

The commandments

The evolution of the trio's business commandments, or principles, is very interesting. First, because it highlights their vision in codifying their culture at a time when no Brazilian companies did so. Second, it shows their humbleness in benchmarking the best aspects of all the cultures that inspired them, something that becomes very clear once one studies Goldman Sachs's business principles, Jack Welch's GE annual reports, and Sam Walton's autobiography: it's all there, in one form or another.

With that in mind, I chose to reproduce my own translation of Banco Garantia's 18 Commandments (and I can assure you I've spent long hours tweaking the wording to get the original Portuguese meanings just right), as well as the current version of AB InBev's 10 business principles (which are really a summary of Garantia's, adapted to the consumer goods arena). I've also chosen to reproduce Goldman's principles, whose influence is clear on the original commandments, and Toyota's 14 principles, which greatly influenced Vicente Falconi, and consequently, AB InBev. I hope you also find these useful.

The process of codifying one's corporate culture is an excruciating one, which in itself highlights the commitment and vision of a company's shareholders and managers. Every one of the cultures that have influenced the trio have some sort of principles list written down. That should be itself an important cue to all businessmen reading this.

Garantia's original 18 commandments

1   A big and challenging dream makes everyone row in the same direction.

2   A company's biggest asset is good people working as a team, growing in proportion to their talent, and being recognized for that. Employee compensation has to be aligned with shareholders' interests.

3   Profits are what attracts investors, people, and opportunities, and keep the wheels spinning.

4   Focus is of the essence. It's impossible to be excellent in everything, so concentrate on the few things that really matter.

5 Everything has to have an owner with authority and accountability. Debate is good, but in the end, someone has to decide.

6 Common sense is as good as fancy concepts. Simple is better than complicated.

7 Transparency and information flow ease decision-making and minimize conflicts.

8 Hiring people who are better than yourself, training them, challenging them, and retaining them is the main attribution of a manager.

9 Leading through example is vital, in both heroic gestures and the simple actions of the company's day-to-day.

10 Luck is always a function of sweat. Work hard, but with joy.

11 Things happen in the business' operations and in the market. You have to pound the pavement.

12 Being paranoid about costs and expenses—the only variables under our control—helps ensure long-term survival.

13 Constant discontent, a sense of urgency, and zero complacency help ensure a sustainable competitive advantage.

14 Innovations that add value are useful, but copying practices that already work is usually easier.

15 Corporate and personal discretion are helpful. Showing off is only allowed when done with concrete objectives.

16 Constant training and improvement have to be ongoing efforts and should permeate our routine.

17 Name, reputation, and brands are precious assets that take decades to build and days to destroy.

18 Trickery and cheating can rot a company from the inside. Ethics pay off on the long run.

AB InBev's 10 Principles

1. Our shared Dream energizes everyone to work in the same direction to be the Best Beer Company Bringing People Together For a Better World.

2. Our greatest strength is our people. Great people grow at the pace of their talent and are rewarded accordingly.

3. We recruit, develop, and retain people who can be better than ourselves. We will be judged by the quality of our teams.

4. We are never completely satisfied with our results, which are the fuel of our company. Focus and zero complacency guarantee lasting competitive advantage.

5. The consumer is the Boss. We serve our consumers by offering brand experiences that play a meaningful role in their lives, and always in a responsible way.

6. We are a company of owners. Owners take results personally.

7 We believe common sense and simplicity are usually better guidelines than unnecessary sophistication and complexity.

8 We manage our costs tightly to free up resources that will support sustainable and profitable top line growth.

9 Leadership by personal example is at the core of our culture. We do what we say.

10 We never take shortcuts. Integrity, hard work, quality, and responsibility are key to building our company.

Goldman Sachs' business principles

1. Our clients' interests always come first.

Our experience shows that if we serve our clients well, our own success will follow.

2. Our assets are our people, capital, and reputation.

If any of these is ever diminished, the last is the most difficult to restore. We are dedicated to complying fully with the letter and spirit of the laws, rules, and ethical principles that govern us. Our continued success depends upon unswerving adherence to this standard.

3. Our goal is to provide superior returns to our shareholders.

Profitability is critical to achieving superior returns, building our capital, and attracting and keeping our best people. Significant employee stock ownership aligns the interests of our employees and our shareholders.

4. We take great pride in the professional quality of our work.

We have an uncompromising determination to achieve excellence in everything we undertake. Though we may be involved in a wide variety and heavy volume of activity, we would, if it came to a choice, rather be best than biggest.

5. We stress creativity and imagination in everything we do.

While recognizing that the old way may still be the best way, we constantly strive to find a better solution to a client's problems. We pride ourselves on having pioneered many of the practices and techniques that have become standard in the industry.

6. We make an unusual effort to identify and recruit the very best person for every job.

Although our activities are measured in billions of dollars, we select our people one by one. In a service business, we know that without the best people, we cannot be the best firm.

7. We offer our people the opportunity to move ahead more rapidly than is possible at most other places.

Advancement depends on merit, and we have yet to find the limits to the responsibility our best people are able to assume. For us to be successful, our men and women must reflect the diversity of the communities and cultures in which we operate. That means we must attract, retain, and motivate people from many backgrounds and perspectives. Being diverse is not optional; it is what we must be.

8. We stress teamwork in everything we do.

While individual creativity is always encouraged, we have found that team effort often produces the best results. We have no room for those who put their personal interests ahead of the interests of the firm and its clients.

9. The dedication of our people to the firm and the intense effort they give their jobs are greater than one finds in most other organizations.

We think that this is an important part of our success.

10. We consider our size an asset that we try hard to preserve.

We want to be big enough to undertake the largest project that any of our clients could contemplate, yet small enough to maintain the loyalty, the intimacy, and the esprit de corps that we all treasure and that contribute greatly to our success.

11. We constantly strive to anticipate the rapidly changing needs of our clients and to develop new services to meet those needs.

We know that the world of finance will not stand still and that complacency can lead to extinction.

12. We regularly receive confidential information as part of our normal client relationships.

To breach a confidence or to use confidential information improperly or carelessly would be unthinkable.

13. Our business is highly competitive, and we aggressively seek to expand our client relationships.

However, we must always be fair competitors and must never denigrate other firms.

14. Integrity and honesty are at the heart of our business.

We expect our people to maintain high ethical standards in everything they do, both in their work for the firm and in their personal lives.

The Toyota Way's 14 Principles

1. Base your management decisions on a long-term philosophy, even at the expense of short-term financial goals.

2. Create a continuous process flow to bring problems to the surface.

3. Use pull systems to avoid overproduction.

4. Level out the workload (heijunka). (Work like the tortoise, not the hare.)

5. Standardized tasks and processes are the foundation for continuous improvement and employee empowerment.

6. Build a culture of stopping to fix problems to get quality right the first time.

7. Use visual control so no problems are hidden.

8. Use only reliable, thoroughly tested technology that serves your people and processes.

9 Grow leaders who thoroughly understand the work, live the philosophy, and teach it to others.

10 Develop exceptional people and teams who follow your company's philosophy.

11 Respect your extended network of partners and suppliers by challenging them and helping them improve.

12 Go and see for yourself to thoroughly understand the situation (genchi genbutsu).

13 Make decisions slowly by consensus, thoroughly considering all options; implement decisions rapidly (nemawashi).

14 Become a learning organization through relentless reflection (hansei) and continuous improvement (kaizen).

BIBLIOGRAPHY

All the videos cited throughout the book are available at the book's website:

http://www.the3Gway.com

There you'll also find other books cited here that will enable you to deepen your understanding of the trio's management culture.

Please also leave the book a review. It is really important to us.

"Acquisitions," on 3G Capital's official website, http://www.3G-Capital.com.

Cohan, William D. *The Last Tycoons*. Doubleday, 2007.

Cohan, William D. *Money and Power*. Anchor, 2011.

Collins, James C. *Good to Great*. Harper Business, 2001.

Collins, James C. *Built to Last*. Harper Business Essentials, 2011.

Correa, Cristiane. *Sonho Grande*. Primeira Pessoa, 2013.

Ellis, Charles D. The Partnership. Penguin Press, 2008.

Falconi Campos, Vicente. *True Power*. Editora Falconi, 2009.

"Investor Relations," on Burger King Holdings' official website, http://investor.bk.com/.

"Investor Relations," on H.J. Heinz Company's official website, http://www.heinz.com/our-company/investor-relations.aspx.

"Investor Relations," on AmBev's official website, http://ri.ambev.com.br

"Investor Relations," on AB InBev's official website, http://ab-inbev.com/go/investors.cfm

"Investor Relations," on Goldman Sachs' official website, http://www.**goldmansachs**.com/ **investor-relations**/

"Investor Relations," on GE's official website, http:// www.**ge**.com/**investor-relations**

"Investor Relations," on Walmart's official website, http://stock.walmart.com

Knoedelseder, William. *Bitter Brew.* Harper Business, 2012.

Liker, Jeffrey R. *The Toyota Way.* McGraw Hill, 2001.

MacIntosh, Julie. *Dethroning the King.* Wiley, 2011.

Neto, Jose Salibi. "O Arquiteto de Empresas," *HSM Management*, number 5, 2001.

Neto, Jose Salibi. "Pensamento Nacional Corporativo: Os 10 Principios de uma Vitoriosa Cultura de Gestão no Brasil," *HSM Management*, number 66, 2008.

Neto, Jose Salibi. "Pensamento Nacional Corporativo: Marcel Telles," *HSM Management*, number 84, 2001.

Schein, Edgar H. *Organizational Culture and Leadership.* Jossey-Bass, 2010.

Serafim, Jacileide de Almeida. "Concepção e Implantação de Grupos Autogerenciáveis: Análise de dois Casos Industriais." Master's thesis, Pontifícia Universidade Católica do Rio de Janeiro, 2005.

Sorkin, Andrew R. *Too Big to Fail.* Viking, 2009.

Teixeira, Alexandre. "O Legado de Lemann," *Época Negócios*, April 2008.

Walton, Samuel Moore, and Huey, John. *Made in America*. Bantam Books, 1993.